SO-AWA-070

VIRTUOUS HEALERS

VIRTUOUS HEALERS

MODELS

OF FAITH

IN MEDICINE

EDGAR A. GAMBOA, M.D., FACS

ST. ANTHONY MESSENGER PRESS
Cincinnati, Ohio

Scripture passages have been taken from *New Revised Standard Version Bible,* copyright ©1989 by the Division of Christian Education of the National Council of the Churches of Christ in the U.S.A., and used by permission. All rights reserved.

Cover design by Mark Sullivan
Cover image © www.istockphoto.com/Kasia Biel
Book design by Jennifer Tibbits

LIBRARY OF CONGRESS CATALOGING-IN-PUBLICATION DATA

Gamboa, Edgar A.
  Virtuous healers : models of faith in medicine / Edgar A. Gamboa.
    p. cm.
  Includes bibliographical references (p.   ).
  ISBN 978-0-86716-693-4 (pbk. : alk. paper) 1. Christian saints—Biography.
2. Catholics—Biography. I. Title.
  BX4655.3.G36 2008
  282.092'2—dc22
  [B]
                                                    2008022485

ISBN 978-0-86716-693-4

Copyright ©2008, Edgar A. Gamboa. All rights reserved.

Published by St. Anthony Messenger Press
28 W. Liberty St.
Cincinnati, OH 45202
www.SAMPBooks.org

Printed in the United States of America.

Printed on acid-free paper.

08 09 10 11 12   5 4 3 2 1

To the millions of idealistic young men and women
around the world—dreamers, thinkers, doers
burning within to dedicate their lives
to the ancient and noble task of alleviating suffering,
saving lives and caring for those taken ill

To Mary, Health of the Sick and Comforter of the Afflicted
And, to Lucie...

CONTENTS

ACKNOWLEDGMENTS | xi

introduction
THE ALPHABET UPRISING | 1

one
HANDS OF GOD:
COMPASSION, KINDNESS AND SYMPATHY | 7
Mother Teresa of Calcutta (1910–1997) | 10

two
TOUGH CHOICES IN THE ICU:
INTEGRITY, ETHICS AND HONESTY | 15
Doctor Gianna Beretta Molla (1922–1962) | 19
Cardinal Joseph Bernardin (1928–1996) | 21

three
LEARNING FROM ATTICUS:
PATIENCE, TOLERANCE AND UNDERSTANDING | 27
Saint Thérèse of Lisieux (Sister Thérèse of the Child Jesus) (1873–1897) | 30

four
SCRUBBING WITH PRAYER:
CONTEMPLATION IN ACTION | 37
Brother Lawrence (1614–1691) | 39
Saint John of God (1495–1550) | 42

five
TAKING A STANCE:
COURAGE AND FORTITUDE | 45
Saint Maximilian Kolbe (1894–1941) | 47
Archbishop Oscar Arnulfo Romero (1917–1980) | 48

six

FRODO'S RING:
HUMILITY AND TEMPERANCE | 53

Blessed Charles de Foucauld (1858–1916) | 56

Blessed Marianne Cope (1838–1918) | 60

seven

KEEPING CODE BLUE GOING:
INITIATIVE, DISCIPLINE,
RESPONSIBILITY AND LEADERSHIP | 63

Doctor Albert Schweitzer (1875–1965) | 64

Saint Elizabeth of Hungary (1207–1231) | 68

eight

LAZARUS ON CHRISTMAS:
HOPE AND PERSEVERANCE | 73

Saint Luke the Evangelist (AD 10–84) | 76

Doctor Tom Dooley (1927–1961) | 78

nine

COFFEE BREAK:
FAITH AND SPIRITUALITY | 87

Saint John of the Cross (1542–1591) | 89

Doctor Adrienne von Speyr (1902–1967) | 93

ten

CHARLIE BROWN AND MANKIND:
HUMANISM, LOVE AND CHARITY | 99

Saint Vincent de Paul (1580–1660) | 100

Saint Camillus de Lellis (1550–1614) | 103

eleven

THE KING'S TREE:

TOTAL TRUST IN DIVINE PROVIDENCE | 107

Saint Teresa of Avila (1515–1582) | 111

Pope John XXIII (1881–1963) | 116

twelve

THE ART OF NOT TAKING ONESELF SERIOUSLY:

SENSE OF HUMOR AND DOWN-TO-EARTH

PRACTICALITY | 123

Saint Philip Neri (1515–1595) | 124

Blessed Artimide Zatti (1880–1951) | 127

thirteen

THE CONSUMMATE PHYSICIAN:

SCIENCE AND RELIGION, TECHNOLOGY AND

SPIRITUALITY, ACADEMICS AND FAITH | 131

Pierre Teilhard de Chardin (1881–1955) | 132

Doctor Alexis Carrel (1873–1944) | 135

fourteen

NO-FRILLS MEDICINE:

SOCIAL JUSTICE AND THE PREFERENTIAL OPTION

FOR THE POOR | 139

Blessed Damien of Molokai (1840–1889) | 142

Dorothy Day (1897–1980) | 145

BIBLIOGRAPHY | 153

INDEX | 158

ACKNOWLEDGMENTS

Very few things, if anything in life, are products of one individual's creativity.

This book traces its origin to Father Tom Santa, C.S.S.R, who in 2000 invited Catholic writers, editors and publishers to come to Picture Rocks, Arizona. Thus was held the first Catholic Writers' Workshop and Retreat in the United States, if not in the world. Vinita Wright, Michael Leach, Charles Roth and Frank Cunningham came to Picture Rocks each year to encourage and inspire rookies and pros to write. Lisa Biedenbach came up with the idea of a spiritual handbook for physicians, nurses and other healthcare professionals.

Many have shown me the relationship between treating the sick, caring for others and loving God. Among them: My wonderful parents, Pedro and Inocencia, my saintly kindergarten teacher, Sor Salvacion, and the Daughters of Charity, the Redemptorists, Padres Paules (Vincentians), the Benedictine monks, the Camaldolese hermits. They also taught me how to pray—especially Father Edward "Bud" Kaicher, Sister Mary Gregory and Father Luke Dougherty—and how to nurture the fading embers of idealism—particularly Fred Dimaya, Father Roque "Khing" Vano, the Honorable Raul S. Manglapus and Doctor Victor Uranga.

It's been a privilege to learn from and to work with many physicians who embody the virtues highlighted in this book. I cannot mention them all but, in random order, my lifelong gratitude goes to: Doctor Nicholas Halasz, Doctor Worthington G. Schenk, Doctor John Border, Doctor Roger Seibel, Doctor Ramon Arcenas, Doctor Gabriel V. Noel, Doctor Mamerto Escano, Doctor Florentino Solon, Doctor Jesus Alvarez, Doctor Tomas Fernandez, Doctor (Sister) Eva Maamo, Doctors Merito and Suga Sotto Yuvienco, Doctors Cesar and Leticia Carabuena, Doctor Francisca Velcek, Doctor Anita Figueredo, Doctor Frank Grabarits, Doctor Fernando Ona, Doctor Nemer Dabage-Forzoli, Doctor Francisco Diaz, Doctor Mahomed Suliman, Doctor Clyde "Bud" Beck, Doctor Christian Mende, Doctor Louis Powers, Doctor J. Alan Berkenfield, Doctor Stuart Eichenfield, Doctor Letty Herrera, Doctor Antonio Garcia, Doctor Jose Paradela, Doctor Peter Halford, Doctor Niall Scully, Doctor David McNaugton, Doctor Tomas Jimenez, Doctor Michael Spector, Doctor Anthony DiBenedetto, Doctor Arnold Migliaccio, Doctor Francisco Tirol, Doctor Robert C. Thomas, Doctor Ramon Pascual, Doctor Roberto Abdelnur, Doctor Guy Yturralde, Doctor Ed Manaig, Doctor Albert Valenzuela, Doctor Pepe Recitas, Doctor Ramy Cadag, Doctor Ed Barcelona, Doctor Stephen DiMarzo and Doctor George Sharpino.

My appreciation and gratitude to friends and family, especially to those who cheerfully endured reviewing the manuscript: Sister Mary Gregory, Father Tom Santa, Father Thomas Matus, Father Thomas Green, Father Alberto Uy, Susan Gazmin Ruiz, Daisy Gonzalez, Helen Zec, Phyllis Baumgart, Christopher Thomas, Doctor Alan Gamboa, Judy Dauber, R.N., and John Paul Gamboa.

Special thanks to Lisa Biedenbach for demonstrating the patience of a saint and to my editor, Mary Hackett, for keeping the pathway lighted. And to Liz McCormack for dutifully Xeroxing as many copies of the manuscript as I needed.

I keep working and walking because of those who love and inspire me: Lucie and our children: Peter-Gabriel, Michael Joseph, Lauren Marie and John Paul.

introduction

THE ALPHABET UPRISING

Healthcare in the United States, beginning in the 1980s, took a sharp turn toward managed care. Experts said the paradigm shift was necessary, even inevitable, to keep the spiraling costs of healthcare down. Medicine had to be efficiently economics-oriented. The traditional three-masted, full-rigged clipper of American medicine had to be replaced with slick speedboats, hastily designed to cruise the medical waters of one of the most pragmatic countries in the world.

For better or worse, the ancient science and art of medicine underwent major surgery—documentation and paperwork superseded diagnosis and treatment; standardized protocols or "recipe medicine" replaced case-by-case clinical decisions; third-party authorization took the place of the bedside physician. Computerized data methodically trimmed down medicine's excess fat, even if such drastic cutting extended deep into vital muscle and bone. The alphabet revolution—HMO, PPO, IPA, DRG—was on.

In the name of economics, the sacred trust between physician and patient was severed, irreparably. Cynicism replaced idealism. A rising wave of anger, frustration and hopelessness swept through the vast medical landscape—in hospitals, clinics and assorted healthcare facilities, affecting not only physicians and nurses, but everyone related to health-care—dentists, pharmacists, therapists, technicians, social workers, clerks.

As the capitalistic culture of a consumer society took over the reins of traditional medicine, doctors, nurses and allied health professionals metamorphosed into an amalgamation of disposable healthcare providers. Patients were digitized, graphed and clustered into a matrix of byte-sized consumers.

The goal of controlling the cost of technologically-driven medicine was justifiable, no doubt, in a GNP-oriented world. Yet, in a process that was primarily dollar-driven, distrust trumped altruism. Feedback was prized over noble intentions. A stark quarterly report carried more value than the warm smile of a grateful patient. Money over mission became the modern mantra. The practice of medicine was systematically dehumanized.

Perhaps, it was inevitable—the healthcare delivery system was due for an upgrade. Wal-Mart and Costco, after all, had replaced mom-and-pop stores across the country. Cinematic megacomplexes had booted the single movie house into oblivion. But, in the chaotic devastation that ensued, frustrated physicians retired early or abandoned the profession in disgust. Some reacted ineffectively, others adapted to the changes in desperation. Faced with skyrocketing malpractice liability insurance and inundated by voluminous paperwork, many physicians burnt out. It did not help that their clinical decisions were increasingly being usurped by nonmedical entities, such as third-party insurers, hospital reviewers and government regulators. In a survey by the California Medical Association, two-thirds of physicians preferred that their children not follow in their footsteps. Applications to medical school dropped by 10,000 or 20 percent.[1]

Yet, sickness takes no holiday. Extended longevity and the geriatric population boom (aging Baby Boomers) ushered in a new set of complicated illnesses which needed to be addressed.

As experienced clinicians shift to other nonmedical endeavors and fewer young men and women enter medical school, who will remain to dedicate their lives to caring for the sick and the dying? Who will rescue premature newborns? Monitor juvenile diabetics? Dialyze renal failure patients? Resuscitate multiple trauma victims?

In a series of essays, anecdotes and reflections, I will attempt to explore the traditional ideals and enduring virtues of the work, the mission, the apostolate that we traditionally call "medicine." Compassion, integrity, patience, fortitude, humility, perseverance, vision, faith, charity, trust, an abiding sense of social justice and—last but not least—a sense of humor are essentials that cannot be discarded from the daily work of medicine. Nor can these characteristics or, if you will, virtues in doctors, nurses and other healthcare professionals and workers be replaced by dispassionate efficiency and pecuniary priorities without, in effect, staining and shredding the delicate fabric of medical practice. Demoting healers to mere providers or reducing suffering patients to blind consumers of economic benefits, as capitalism does, cheapens human interaction, just as making robots of human beings, as shown in the Communist experiment, mechanizes it.

I speak with some degree of experience, from the vantage point of one who spent eleven years (1976–1987) in residency training, fellowship programs and academic surgery in New York and California, following medical school and postgraduate internship in the Philippines (1970–1976). By happenstance, I have spent twenty years (1988–2008) in clinical surgical practice, solo or with multi-specialty groups, in a variety of clinical practice settings—inner city, suburb, rural, coastal, desert, island—from the most affluent to the poorest communities. In over thirty years, I have treated all kinds of patients and have seen the many faces of medicine, both in the United States and on international medical missions.

Since early childhood, I have been, like most kids in Catholic schools, fascinated with the lives of the saints. I looked upon those heroic men and women as beyond human, in the league of Batman and Superman, though leaning more on the spiritual side, of course. As I got older, I realized how truly human they were—confronted with the same problems we face, struggling through similar obstacles, sorting out familiar dilemmas. Yet somehow, through God's grace and their faithfulness and trust, the saints emerged through life with a special glow. This struck me as I knelt on the worn-out pew that was Dorothy Day's favorite, as I stood in Saint Romuald's simple cell, and as I viewed Saint Padre Pio's ordinary-looking confessional.

How would the saints, if they were in our shoes today, solve the problems we are confronted with? Not an easy question to answer, admittedly. But I figured that sketching the lives of some of these heroic men and women who were physicians, nurses, hospital attendants, or involved in one way or another with medicine and caring for the sick may bring us closer to an answer.

Many saints spoke only with their actions. But some expressed views relevant to our present situation. Addressing doctors specifically, Mother Teresa said:

> Yours is a consecrated life, because touching the sick, in healing the sick, Jesus said: 'You did it to me'[2]
>
> ....Yours is not only a profession but a vocation – the vocation to be God's love, Gods' compassion, God's healing power to the suffering. God has chosen you for a special mission. Being a doctor means going out and touching God in each of the suffering, whether it be the rich or the poor, for sickness strikes all.[3]
>
> ...[B]efore you touch a patient, before you listen to the patient—pray. Because you need a clean heart to love that patient. And you need clean hands to touch that patient...Through this work of your hands and heart you may grow

in holiness. Let us promise our Lord that through your medical work, you are going to become holy.[4]

Mother Teresa also pleaded to medical students:

I beg of you not to add to the millions of doctors already present who are just doling out medicines. You must treat each patient with love and compassion and fulfill all the hopes they come with. Your hands are instruments of peace and are used to restore life…[5]

Selecting which saints to highlight was no easy task. All of them are special and interesting personalities; each one worth studying. But since I'm not writing an encyclopedia (thank God), I've limited the hagiography to icons such as: Mother Teresa of Calcutta; human rights activist Dorothy Day who, I was delighted to discover, served a nursing stint at a hospital in Brooklyn, New York, where I had trained; Joseph Cardinal Bernardin, the late Archbishop of Chicago, who, when diagnosed with unresectable pancreatic cancer, shifted his focus from his terminal condition to ministering to fellow cancer patients.

My focus on Catholic holy people should in no way imply that medicine's ideals are best exemplified, much less restricted, to Christianity. It simply means that I have more familiarity with personalities who made a difference in my faith tradition. It goes without saying that medicine is as old as humanity itself and history attests to the fact that men and women through the ages, from all cultural backgrounds and spiritual traditions—Judaism, Islam, Buddhism, Hinduism, Taoism, Confucianism, to name but a few—have given extraordinary expression to medicine's purest ideals.

The reader will find points for reflection or discussion at the end of each chapter. Exercises are given as mere suggestions. It would be beneficial if the book is read one or two chapters at a time, and not necessarily in sequence. Read in this manner, the reader's own reflection may lead to more personalized exercises and practical resolutions. Relevant prayers conclude each chapter. This handbook may also serve as material for group study and discussion.

Going back to the medical crisis we are currently immersed in, Bob Dylan's 1964 ballad may lend some perspective: "The times they are a-changin." We may not see the current dark cloud of medicine lift in our lifetime. But this too will pass. As men and women entrusted with the noble mission of caring for fellow human beings taken ill or suffering, let it not be said that, in the midst of darkness, our spirits were broken and our collective resolve vanquished. Rather, let it be known that, dedicated and faithful to our God-given vocation, and inspired by the example of heroic men and women who came before us, we gently placed stethoscopes on our patients' chests, carried our crosses courageously, and kept the light of medicine burning brightly for the next generations.

notes

[1] Katherine Hobson, "Doctors Vanish From View," *U.S. News & World Report*, January 23, 2005.

[2] Jaya Chalika and Edward Le Joly, *Mother Teresa: The Joy in Living: A Guide to Daily Living*, (Penguin, 1996), p. 344.

[3] Chalika and Le Joly, p. 74.

[4] Chalika and Le Joly, p. 352.

[5] Chalika and Le Joly, p. 194.

one

HANDS OF GOD

Compassion, Kindness and Sympathy

At the end of our lives, we will not be judged by how many diplomas we have received, how much money we have made or how many great things we have done. We will be judged by "I was hungry and you gave me to eat. I was naked and you clothed me. I was homeless and you took me in."....[The patient in front of us] is Christ in distressing disguise.[1]

—MOTHER TERESA OF CALCUTTA

When you left the hallowed walls of academia, didn't you feel as adventurous as Don Quixote in the *Man of La Mancha*? Bring me the poor, the sick, the suffering. Bring them on! I will treat them all. I will venture into the slums of the inner city, seek the remotest village, cross the wildest rivers—if that is what it takes to treat the sick and the dying.

Fast forward a few years. You are a haggard senior resident, awake all night tending to a septic multiple organ failure patient in the ICU, or resuscitating major trauma patients rescued from a rollover car crash. It's 2 AM and the ER triage nurse tells you there is a "frequent flyer" in Room 2, could you give him a prescription for Vicodin and, while at it, examine the fungating ulcer in his foot? You give her a cold stare and say, "Get that dirtbag out of here!"

What happened in the intervening years? Did you finally learn how to be a real doctor? Practical, efficient, savvy? Or have constant clashes with reality taken their toll? Did the fire of compassion, once burning so passionately in your idealistic soul, finally flicker out?

You look back and realize with some degree of horror that you have conveniently forgotten the fact that Mr. Jerry Regado's wife walked out on him a year ago; he found solace in alcohol till the auto shop owner had enough of his hangovers and kicked him out. Mr. Regado is the frequent flyer in Room 2, the guy who just does not know how to keep his leg clean, the *loser* who lives for his pain meds. Through years of working protracted hours, hectic nights and disrupted dinners, you have learned to tag patients as medical record number 12-34-56 or the gallbladder in Room 201, the bowel obstruction in the ICU, the kidney stone getting an IVP in x-ray, or the stroke undergoing an MRI.

The hospital system has not helped either. Utilization wonders why the "census" is down. Discharge planners ask why we couldn't move "bodies" out early enough. Even the insurance companies brag that they are responsible for half of the "clients in your area," or that they secure "35,000 lives" in their files. Practice consultants remind you it is important to update your "consumers" on billing policies.

Forget about the sick, the suffering and the dying. It's the twenty-first century—think "consumers," "HMO lives," "medical record numbers," "census stats," "frequent flyers," "gallbladders," "cardiacs," "ulcers," "GOMERS" (ER acronym for "Get Out of My Emergency Room").

The ultimate shock comes when the triage nurse tells you to finish your sandwich quickly so you can evaluate the "dirtbag" in the holding cubicle. And, wiping the mustard from your lips, you ask her if she's referring to dirtbag *one* or *two*!

Yet treating your fellow human beings in pain and suffering—whether their ailments are self-inflicted or accidental, genetic or a consequence of poor behavior, whether the people themselves are crazy or sane, educated or illiterate, emotionally adjusted or obnoxious, able to pay for your services or not—is what you went to medical school for.

Treating patients, alleviating their suffering, healing them, curing them, saving their lives—this is why you stayed up past midnight, reviewing the intricacies of *Gray's Anatomy*, the complexities of renal physiology, the maze of diagnostic algorithms. This is why you memorized the Latin names of thousands of bacteria and viruses, and the corresponding chemicals which weakened or smashed their cells. This is why you canceled a weekend date, so you could spend Saturday night learning to interpret the spikes of an EKG. This is why you gave up sun and sea to spend your residency in Buffalo, New York (where the seasons are winter and July), so you would learn the surgical techniques that saved people from the devastating encroachments of cancer and the lethal effects of a head-on car collision. This is why you sat yawning from one lecture to the next, so you would learn acid-base balance and fluid resuscitation and recognize when patients started to third space.

And now you find yourself, at 2 AM, weary, tired, sleep-deprived, wishing you did not have to bother with the schizophrenic belly pain who's cursing the nurses and yelling for a shot of morphine.

Still you have chosen a profession that begs you to dig deep into the inner core of your soul and reclaim your tarnished ideals. The friendly hospital chaplain says you did not choose medicine; rather you were chosen (and from all eternity) to be God's instrument of healing. You literally have become the hands of God. So, why complain? Would you rather be doing something else with your life?

A VIRTUOUS HEALER WHO EXEMPLIFIED COMPASSION, KINDNESS AND SYMPATHY

Mother Teresa of Calcutta
(1910–1997)

I never look at the masses as my responsibility. I look only at the individual. I can love only one person at a time. I can feed only one person at a time. Just one, one, one.... The whole work is only a drop in the ocean. But if we don't put the drop in, the ocean would be one drop less.[2]

—MOTHER TERESA OF CALCUTTA

Mother Teresa of Calcutta, Founder of the Missionaries of Charity, was one person who dug deep into her soul, bringing forth an encompassing sense of compassion for the suffering person. In loving the person entrusted to her care, she radiated the love of Christ.

"Let anyone who comes to you go away feeling better and happier. Every one should see goodness in your face, in your eyes, in your smile."[3]

Born in Skopje, Macedonia, on August 26, 1910, Agnes Gonxha was the youngest of the three children of Albanians Nikola and Drana Bojaxhiu. The future advocate for the poorest of the poor did not grow up in poverty, as Nikola ran a successful business. When Nikola died, Drana supported her family by merchandising embroidery and carpets. She was an exemplary woman of faith, who inculcated in her children social awareness and concern for the needs of others. Drana gathered her children every evening to pray the rosary. She brought her daughters on pilgrimages to the shrine of Our Lady of Cernagore in Montenegro.

Agnes Gonxha was educated in a state-run secondary school in Croatia. Inspired to pursue missionary work in India by the letters of Jesuit priest, Father Anthony Vizjak, she joined the Order of Loreto in Dublin on September 25, 1928, and adopted the name of Saint Thérèse of Lisieux, patroness of the missions. On May 14, 1937, Sister Teresa took her final vows of poverty, chastity and obedience. Her superiors assigned her to Calcutta to teach at a boarding school run by the congregation. Learning to speak Bengali and Hindi, the young Sister Teresa taught geography and history and later became headmistress of Saint Mary's High School. But working at a privileged private school, an affluent enclave in the midst of widespread poverty, bothered her. On September 10, 1946, aboard a train on the way to Darjeeling in the Himalayas for her annual retreat, the thirty-six-year-old Sister Teresa received what she later referred to as a "call within a call":

> I was going to Darjeeling to make my retreat.... It was on that train that I heard the call to give up all and follow Him into the slums—to serve Him in the poorest of the poor. I knew it was His will and I had to follow Him. There was no doubt it was to be His work.... The message was quite clear. I was to leave the convent and work with the poor while living among them. It was an order. I knew where I belonged, but I did not know how to get there.[4]

Granted permission by her superiors, Sister Teresa petitioned the Archbishop of Calcutta for "exclaustration," or the ability to live and carry out her mission outside her congregation while remaining faithful to her religious vows. She felt it was not enough to help the poor from a distance. It was necessary to be among them, to experience their way of life firsthand, thereby understanding and effectively ministering to their needs. She knew well that in order for "Love to be real, it must cost—it must hurt—it must empty us of self."[5] She requested her spiritual director to bless a sari, a cross and a rosary—the rudimentary and symbolic instruments of the work she envisioned among the homeless and the slum dwellers of Calcutta.

It was a time of turmoil and crisis in colonial India. The British Empire had dragged India into World War II and the sweltering city of Calcutta was inundated by refugees. Under the leadership of Mohandas

Gandhi, the nascent nonviolent resistance movement against the British had gained traction.

Pope Pius XII granted Mother Teresa's petition to work as an exclaustrated nun on April 12, 1948. Trading her cherished Loreto habit for the traditional outfit of a poor Bengali (white sari and sandals), Mother Teresa traveled to Patna, where she trained at the hospital of the American Medical Missionary Sisters.

At the Holy Family Hospital, Mother Teresa quickly learned basic medical knowledge and developed nursing skills, such as preparing hospital beds, taking vital signs and administering injections. She learned to deliver babies as well, preparatory to serving the poorest of the poor.

Thereafter, she started working in the slum districts and in February 1949 set up her mission in a room of a three-story colonial house. People were drawn to the house at 14 Creek Street and began to help Mother Teresa care for the poor and the sick. Under her direction, volunteers, including some of her students at Saint Mary's school, sought children in the poorest areas of the city and people dying in city streets.

Mother Teresa's centers for the homeless, abandoned men and women, malnourished children, dying HIV patients, lepers and others, spread throughout the world. By the 1990s, such centers of loving care and compassion grew to over six hundred houses in 136 countries.

On her trips abroad, when people asked to join her work in Calcutta, Mother Teresa would graciously invite them to visit Calcutta but advised prospective volunteers to "Find your own Calcutta.... Don't search for God in far lands—he is not there. He is close to you, he is with you. Just keep the lamp burning and you will always see him."[6]

Mother Teresa received the Nobel Peace Prize in 1979. Despite her many accolades and honors, she remained humble and kept her sense of humor. When someone asked her, "What will you do when you are not

Mother General any more?" She thought for a while, smiled, and said, "I am first-class at cleaning toilets and drains."[7]

Mother Teresa was beatified by Pope John Paul II in October 2003.

QUESTIONS FOR REFLECTION

1. Does the image of Quixote's *Man of La Mancha* still apply to you? Can you still picture yourself jousting imaginary windmills? Or have the passing years encrusted your childhood dreams, blunted your optimism, watered down your idealism?

2. Once upon a time, didn't you dream of eradicating disease, hunger and suffering? Didn't you enter medical or nursing school excited about the prospect of saving lives, changing the world and making a difference?

3. When you graduated, weren't you convinced you had found your life's calling, vocation and mission? Why do you now feel such relief turning off your beeper or cell phone and so much happiness to leave the hospital or the clinic?

4. Have your goals and priorities changed through the years? Do you feel you have paid a heavy price to achieve your goals?

SPIRITUAL EXERCISE

Envision the suffering Christ in the next patient you treat in the hospital or in your clinic. Lay your hands on Christ's battered body, cleanse his wounds and gently take off the crown of thorns. Listen to what he has to say. Comfort him. Observe how that vision may transform the way you care for that particular patient. Write a brief description of that sacred encounter in your diary or spend some time reflecting on the experience.

PRAYER

Eternal Word, only begotten Son of God,
Teach me true generosity.
Teach me to serve you as you deserve.

To give without counting the cost,

To fight without heeding the wounds,

To labor without seeking rest,

To sacrifice myself without thought of any reward

Save the knowledge that I have done your will.

Amen.

—Attributed to Saint Ignatius Loyola

notes

[1] Michael Collopy, *Works of Love are Works of Peace: Mother Teresa of Calcutta and the Missionaries of Charity* (San Francisco: Ignatius, 1996), p. 35.

[2] Collopy, p. 35.

[3] Chalika and Le Joly, p. 105.

[4] Roger Royle, *Mother Teresa: A Life in Pictures* (San Francisco: HarperSanFrancsico, 1992), p. 21.

[5] Collopy, p. 30.

[6] Robert Ellsberg, *All Saints: Daily Reflections on Saints, Prophets, and Witnesses of Our Time* (New York: Crossroad, 1997), pp. 393–394.

[7] Chalika and Le Joly, p. 345.

t w o

TOUGH CHOICES IN THE ICU

Integrity, Ethics and Honesty

"In the same way, let your light shine before others, so that they may
see your good works and give glory to your Father in heaven."

—MATTHEW 5:16

People at times complain about physicians "playing God," the implication
being that doctors try to control the levers of life and death. Families of
dying patients resent doctors who seem to have little, if any regard, for
the far-reaching consequences of their *ex cathedra* decisions.

Yet, in reality, nothing can be further from the truth. It is the rare
physician who does not agonize when patients take a turn for the worse.
Granted, physicians may fail to sit down (not infrequently due to their
hectic schedules) and give families the extra time they need to change
gears and begin to accept the painful reality of impending loss. Doctors
also find it particularly difficult to face defeat and they dislike lingering
when death becomes inevitable—an attitude families may misinterpret as
callousness.

Each patient is unique. But the following case may serve to point out
the intricacies involved in making decisions in the ICU.

Mr. D was a seventy-eight-year-old retired maintenance man. For decades, he had worked behind the scenes, mainly in hospitals, fixing and keeping machines functional so that doctors and nurses could go about their daily work of saving lives. Mr. D had the highest regard for the medical and nursing professions.

He had survived lung cancer and in his twilight years he enjoyed traveling and visiting his grandchildren. It was during one of these family visits that he fell ill. The doctor south of the border thought he had appendicitis and recommended an operation. Mr. D decided to return to the United States and came to our ER.

He complained of upper and lower abdominal pain so the ER physician ordered a CT scan because he was not sure if Mr. D had appendicitis, a cholecystitis (gallbladder infection), or a pancreatitis (inflammation of the pancreas, the small organ located behind the stomach). I was asked to consult. After examining him and reviewing the CT scan, it looked like his primary problem was biliary, that is, gallstones plugging the gallbladder. He needed an operation.

Mr. D's cardiac history was vague and his EKG was abnormal so I called in our cardiologist to clear him for surgery—to check whether his heart was healthy enough to withstand anesthesia and carry him through major surgery. The cardiologist reviewed the EKG and declared him a high risk for any major operation. Mr. D would have to undergo cardiac stress testing and a battery of tests before he could be cleared to proceed with surgery. If we took the chance, he might die on the operating table.

After explaining the situation to Mr. D and his family and going over different options available, we decided to defer the operation and treat him with broad-spectrum intravenous antibiotics. The goal was to cool down the infection and relieve his pain, while carrying out more definitive cardiac testing.

The antibiotics worked wonderfully for a few days; his white count (an indicator of severity of infection) fell, his fever came down and his abdominal pain lessened. However, the cardiologist could not clear him for surgery; thus, we requested our radiologist to direct a thin catheter into the gallbladder with CT scan guidance so that infected bile could be drained, temporarily avoiding major surgery. Utilizing local anesthesia, the minor procedure would not put him at risk.

The drain worked, and Mr. D improved. But, after a few days, his white count rose and he became acutely ill. Conservative treatment was not good enough; this time he needed an operation, though he certainly could still die on the operating table or soon after surgery. Should we take our chances?

Again, we sat down with Mr. D and his family. Despite the risk of a myocardial infarction which could lead to cardiac arrest, or pulmonary failure which could mean prolonged use of a respirator, surgery was the only option left. For the better part of his life, Mr. D had worked in hospitals. He trusted doctors and nurses. Whatever we thought reasonable was good enough for him, he told his family. God would take care of the rest.

The operation went smoothly. His heart hardly faltered. His blood pressure remained relatively steady. The gallbladder, as we anticipated, was badly infected. In addition, he appeared to harbor terminal ileitis (Crohn's disease) accounting for his lower abdominal pain. Everyone was relieved that the operation was a success. Post-operatively, Mr. D had to be put on a respirator so we could "keep him down" with high doses of sedation and pain medication, minimizing any strain to his delicate heart.

Forty-eight hours after surgery, however, Mr. D got restless and "extubated" himself—he pulled out his endotracheal (windpipe) tube and disconnected himself from the respirator. The ICU intensivist and pulmologist thought of reinserting the tube but Mr. D maintained adequate levels of oxygen and it was better to let him breathe on his own if he were capable.

Twelve hours later, his oxygen levels fell and he slid into respiratory failure. His heart stopped and CPR was conducted for nine minutes. Reconnected to the respirator, his oxygenation was fine. Surprisingly, his heart, which was inactive for at least ninety seconds, appeared to recover. A few hours later, however, the ICU nurse noted that Mr. D was not reacting; he was not waking up as expected. During the arrest, his brain had suffered critically from lack of oxygen. While his brain stem was still working (maintaining his vital signs), he was not conscious. A CT scan of the brain did not show cerebral edema (swelling) or intracranial hemorrhage (bleeding). He was not "brain dead" but he was not waking up either.

Was this coma a temporary situation from which Mr. D would eventually recover? A neurologist was consulted and he felt that the brain damage (cerebral anoxia) was irreversible. So did the intensivist. The internist and I, on the other hand, felt that given time there was a chance he would recover. This brought us to the stark realization of how little we know about brain physiology, despite advances in many other areas of medical science.

Unlike the human heart, which by EKG, echogram and angiogram, we can examine well enough to predict treatment outcomes, diagnostic imaging of the brain by CT, PET scan or MRI, with the aim of predicting viability or function is still relatively primitive.

I persuaded Mr. D's family to give it some time. They were understandably distraught. While some held on, hoping for the best, others were worried about how long he was going to "suffer" on the respirator, while still others were concerned about funeral arrangements. Even the ICU nurses were divided, some anticipating that we would perform a tracheotomy (an opening in the windpipe) in preparation for prolonged ventilation and eventual recovery, while others wondered if our efforts were futile.

It is precisely for difficult situations such as these that ethics committees have been organized in many hospitals. Family members, medical and nursing staff, the hospital chaplain and social workers meet and review the patient's clinical course, treatment options and prognosis. Coming from various ethical and religious backgrounds, it is often not easy even for well-intentioned and conscientious individuals to reach a consensus.

There are guidelines for deciding if a person is brain dead—for example, a brain-flow study, which is done for purposes of organ donation. There are also ethical guidelines for not pursuing extraordinary measures—prolonged ventilation, renal dialysis—to keep terminally ill patients alive.

These look clean cut and easy on paper. It is an altogether different scenario when, adhering to our primary mission of saving lives, we attempt to guide an often divided family through painful, emotion-laden choices: "do everything possible," "stay the course," "do not resuscitate," "stop the ventilator."

Grappling with such complex situations, we may often discover the inner, deeper chambers of our souls.

 VIRTUOUS HEALERS WHO EXEMPLIFIED
INTEGRITY, ETHICS AND HONESTY

Doctor Gianna Beretta Molla
(1 9 2 2 – 1 9 6 2)

"Look at the mothers who truly love their children—how many sacrifices they make for them. They are ready for everything...."
—GIANNA BERETTA MOLLA

Italian pediatrician Doctor Gianna Beretta Molla could be someone to look up to when faced with unexpected illness or with difficult life-

and-death decisions. Born in Magenta, near Milan, Italy, on October 4, 1922, Doctor Molla attended medical school at the University of Milan and the University of Pavia, graduating in 1949 at age twenty-seven. In 1952, she received a specialty certification in pediatrics and opened a clinic in Mesero. Three years later, after a life-changing pilgrimage to Lourdes, she met engineer Pietro Molla. Their happy marriage produced three children—Pierluigi, Maria Zita and Laura. Gianna loved her family and her profession; she also had a passion for skiing and mountain hiking.

Tragedy struck in 1961 when Doctor Gianna was diagnosed with uterine fibroma and an ovarian tumor during the first trimester of her fourth pregnancy. Due to the high risks associated with carrying the pregnancy to full term, her obstetricians recommended a therapeutic abortion, but Doctor Gianna refused. She would undergo surgery only on the condition that the life of her fourth child be spared at all cost. Terminating a high-risk pregnancy would have been the easy way out but Doctor Gianna valued the life of her unborn baby over her own. She instructed her physician, "If you must decide between me and the child, do not hesitate. Choose the child—I insist on it. Save the baby."[1] Eventually assured by her physicians that her baby's life would not be compromised, Doctor Gianna underwent surgery to resect the ovarian tumor. On Holy Saturday, April 28, 1962, a week after the birth of her daughter, Gianna Emanuela, Doctor Gianna developed postpartum sepsis (overwhelming infection) and died.

A miracle attributed to her intercession was reported by an expectant mother who had sustained a placental tear with consequent loss of amniotic fluid during her second trimester. At risk of dying from sepsis, Elisabeth Comparini Arcolino, mother of three children, was advised by her physicians to undergo a therapeutic abortion. However, after consulting with the Bishop of Franca in Brazil, she prayed to Gianna for guidance and chose to carry the pregnancy to term. On May 31, 2000, Elisabeth Arcolino successfully underwent a Caesarian section and delivered a healthy baby girl, later baptized Gianna Maria in honor of the future saint.

Doctor Gianna Beretta Molla was beatified on April 24, 1994 with her husband Pietro and their thirty-two-year-old daughter, Gianna Emmanuela Molla, attending the ceremony. A devoted wife and mother, an exemplary pediatrician, and an inspiration to the pro-life movement, Doctor Gianna was declared a saint on May 16, 2004, by Pope John Paul II. She is the first married laywoman and female physician to be canonized, exemplifying the Second Vatican Council's precept that the invitation to holiness is a unique call to each and every individual, whether religious or secular.

Cardinal Joseph Bernardin
(1 9 2 8 – 1 9 9 6)

"The truth is that each life is of infinite value…a gift that flows from the very being of God and is entrusted to each of us."

—CARDINAL JOSEPH BERNARDIN

Of Italian descent but born and raised in the United States (his parents, Joseph and Maria Bernardin, emigrated from northern Italy), Joseph Bernardin was, like Saint Gianna, passionate about the unique value and sacredness of human life. As general secretary and then as president of the United States Conference of Catholic Bishops, Bernardin led his fellow bishops in shaping and communicating a pro-life message to the church in America and the whole world.

Chairing the USCCB Ad Hoc Committee on War and Peace, Bernardin, then Archbishop of Cincinnati, was instrumental in drafting *The Challenge of Peace: God's Promise and Our Response*, the pastoral letter which questioned the morality of nuclear warfare and the prevailing policy of deterrence. It was the then-called National Conference of Catholic

Bishop's (NCCB) farthest reaching document ever on public policy and it sparked an international debate which *TIME* magazine covered in its November 29, 1982, issue, featuring Bernardin on its cover.[2] Cardinal Bernardin linked the infinite value of human life to our day-to-day responsibilities and, shortly after being appointed archbishop of Chicago and elevated to the college of cardinals by Pope John Paul II, he began to speak about a "consistent ethic of life."[3] Comparing ethics to a "seamless garment,"[4] Cardinal Bernardin envisioned an integrated pro-life approach, nurtured by a spirit of peace and social justice. In contrast to selective or patchwork ethics, Cardinal Bernardin articulated "seamless" and consistent ethics, which would be ideal in approaching a wide variety of complex moral issues dealing with the fundamental questions of life, such as abortion, euthanasia, capital punishment, military campaigns and nuclear warfare. In Bernardin's seamless view, one cannot be pro-life and endorse capital punishment. Nor can one be pro-abortion and be anti-war.

Joseph Bernardin's early ambition was to become a physician. He enrolled at the University of South Carolina where he was granted a scholarship. He once said, "I decided to enter the pre-med program. It seemed to me that becoming a doctor would be a noble endeavor, enabling me to help people and at the same time provide the means to live a secure life. But God had different plans for me."[5] A year later, following several discussions with priests in his parish, he transferred to Saint Mary's College in Kentucky, Saint Mary's Seminary in Baltimore and then to the Catholic University of America in Washington, D.C., to study for the priesthood. He was ordained for the diocese of Charleston on April 26, 1952.

In 1959, Pope John XXIII named Joseph Bernardin a papal chamberlain. In 1966, at age thirty-eight, Bernardin became the youngest bishop in the United States when Pope Paul VI appointed him Auxiliary

Bishop of the Archdiocese of Atlanta. He was appointed archbishop of Cincinnati in 1972.

Bishop Bernardin was a tireless advocate for peace and social justice, frequently speaking out against violence in war-torn areas, such as Lebanon, Israel and Northern Ireland. He was deeply involved in ecumenical and interfaith dialogues. Well-known for breaking barriers and reaching out to the marginalized, he was the first to offer a Mass for divorced and separated Catholics at Holy Name Cathedral and one of the first to set up an AIDS task force in 1985.

Cardinal Bernardin adopted a firm stance on clerical abuse cases. The reforms he implemented in his archdiocese served as a model across the nation. In 1993, Cardinal Bernardin was himself falsely accused of sexual abuse. He promptly requested a full and impartial investigation and subjected himself to the same rigorous process he had initiated in his archdiocese for such cases. He willingly met with the press and courageously faced a barrage of embarrassing questions, while serenely maintaining his innocence. Three months into the much-publicized ordeal, Cardinal Bernardin was cleared of the charges when his accuser retracted his claims and apologized. Cardinal Bernardin then met with and forgave his accuser.

In 1995, Cardinal Bernardin was diagnosed with and underwent surgery for pancreatic cancer. Not quite fully recovered after being discharged from the hospital, he initiated a cancer ministry, tirelessly making rounds to comfort fellow cancer patients, even as he was undergoing therapy himself. Bernardin's compassion, kindness and personal strength touched the lives of countless patients, many of whom wrote to thank him.

In September 1996 Joseph Cardinal Bernardin was awarded the Presidential Medal of Freedom. He was lauded for his work and commitment to racial equality, arms control and social justice. Among his fellow recipients was civil rights pioneer Rosa Parks.

Approaching his final days, Cardinal Bernardin wrote to the United States Supreme Court to encourage the justices to oppose physician-assisted suicide. With joy and peace, as profoundly expressed in his demeanor, in his words and in his final writings, Cardinal Joseph Bernardin died at the age of sixty-eight on November 14, 1996.

QUESTIONS FOR REFLECTION

1. Do you take the extra time and effort to explain your patient's clinical situation to his or her family?
2. Do you try to fully understand your patients and their family's concerns? Or do you get irritated by seemingly irrelevant questions?
3. When faced with complex ethical decisions do you get the patient's family together and facilitate a consensus? Do you call in the ethics committee? Or do you prefer to confront tough issues yourself?

SPIRITUAL EXERCISE

Place yourself in the position of the son or daughter of Mr. D who were overwhelmed by the unexpected situation in the ICU. What would you do for a beloved family member in the same situation? How would you handle the difficult decision? How would you want someone to handle the situation if you were the one in the coma?

PRAYER

Create in me a clean heart, O God,
    and put a new and right spirit within me.
Do not cast me away from your presence,
    and do not take your holy spirit from me.
—Psalm 51:10–11

notes

[1] Tom Rosica, *Saint Gianna Beretta Molla*, Catholic Insight, December 3, 2006 available at http://catholicinsight.com/online/saints/stmolla.shtml.

[2] Archives Archdiocese of Chicago. Biography of Joseph Cardinal Bernardin, p. 2, at http://archives.archchicago.org/jcbbio.htm.

[3] John Bookser Feister. "Cardinal Joseph L. Bernardin: Didn't He Show Us the Way?" *Saint Anthony Messenger* Magazine, February, 1997.

[4] Feister.

[5] Cardinal Joseph Bernardin, *The Gift of Peace: Personal Reflections* (New York: Doubleday, 1998), p. 85.

three

LEARNING FROM ATTICUS

Patience, Tolerance and Understanding

*"But I say to you, Do not resist an evildoer. But if anyone strikes you
on the right cheek, turn the other also; and if anyone wants to sue you
and take your coat, give your cloak as well; and if anyone forces you
to go one, go also the second mile. Give to everyone who begs from
you, and do not refuse anyone who wants to borrow from you. "*

—MATTHEW 5:39–43

Rudy, the patient in Room 203, was from out of town. Married just over
a year ago to his high school sweetheart and expecting their first baby, he
had just secured a new job. They were ready to move out of his parent's
house, and settle into their new apartment in the big city.

But this Thanksgiving weekend, he was one of a hundred thousand
revelers enjoying the popular sand dunes east of San Diego in Imperial
Valley. Rudy recalled the sustained adrenaline rush, starting with the
preparations for the weekend getaway, tuning up the motorbikes, pack-
ing the camping gear, filling the ice chest with beer, joining the long
parade of desert rats to the wide expanse of nature, cool nights, silent
stars above and crackling bonfires below. What a life!

He was one of the first to get up that morning. He revved up the new dirt bike. What a sound. The roar of the fine-tuned engine was music to his ears. Vroooommmmm. He put on his helmet and his leather jacket and off he went, testing sand and wind, challenging Mother Nature's whims. Facing the morning sun, Rudy caught a glimpse of a group of bike riders trekking up a hillside. It looked like a good place to start. Perfect for a quick surge and landing. He studied the hill one more time...perfect. He stepped on the gas and accelerated. Vvooosshhh...he was up in the air and then quickly looked down for a landing spot. But he had miscalculated. He had not seen the thirty-foot gap. Bam! The impact threw him in the air and he landed hard on his left shoulder and flank.

He could hardly breathe. Briefly, he saw stars. The pain to his side was excruciating. Then he passed out.

He woke up in a busy ER. Doctors, nurses and technicians were hovering over him while checking his pulse and asking him to take a deep breath. One tech took an X ray while a nurse poked his arm with a needle. The pain in his side was throbbing. It felt like some madman was repeatedly stabbing him with a very long knife.

These types of severe trauma are common during the winter and the hospital is geared to treating them according to a standardized trauma protocol—chest X rays, CT scans, O_2 monitoring, telemetry, serial hemoglobins and hematocrits, ER to ICU management.

The ER doctor assured Rudy that everything was going to be all right. He had fractured his jaw and broken five ribs, a wrist and an ankle. He needed to stay in the hospital, of course. "How long?" Rudy blurted. About a week or so. Then it hit him. What about his new job, would he lose it? His wife, what if she delivered this week? The apartment, would they lose it? Will insurance cover all the expenses? Another nurse came by, gave him a shot of morphine and told him to relax. Did he want his family called?

On call, I rushed to the trauma bay and reassessed him. His bleeding had slowed. The chest tube had expanded his collapsed lung. But the entire left side of the chest was crushed. He would benefit from a PCA (pump-controlled pain medicine), but he needed to be watched closely in the ICU, his oxygen exchange monitored. I would check him again after I had finished operating on the liver laceration patient who was getting wheeled into the OR.

Three hours later, when I got out of the OR, the unit secretary was frantic, the nurses were anxious, the patient's wife was furious. Why didn't anyone call her immediately after the accident? Where was the surgeon? Why was he not at the bedside, as he should be, attending to her husband's injuries? Didn't the doctors realize her husband was in such agony? Why didn't the surgeon call her and explain the extent of his injuries? Were the nurses giving her husband enough pain medicine?

It would help if doctors could bilocate, like Saint Pio of Pietrelcina. I could attend to the liver laceration in the operating room while simultaneously monitoring the patient in the ICU, and comforting his wife, mother, aunt and stepbrother.

Rudy was seriously injured, but he was one of five other multiple trauma patients who needed our attention. Yet, he was the only sick person in the hospital that mattered to his family. His wife ranted and raved. Wasn't it obvious to everyone that her husband was hovering between life and death? The medical and nursing staff were either oblivious to the situation or did not care enough to focus their full attention on her husband. I did not find out until later that the young wife was experiencing a difficult pregnancy and her husband's accident had tipped the balance. She was worried that her husband would be disabled and was horrified at the consequences. While the medical and nursing staffs considered Rudy a routine trauma case, one of a dozen we were going to treat that weekend, she thought her world had totally collapsed.

Fortunately, cases of an uncontrollable spouse, over-solicitous parent, an impossible son or daughter, are few and far between. But they do happen, most often when there's a family history of unresolved conflict and neglect. And when such cases come to the scene, the staff's clinical focus gets diverted to facing emotional outbursts and repetitive queries. It is during such trying circumstances that physicians and nurses often need to ask for the grace of patience, compassion and understanding.

Sometimes, I take comfort in recalling what Atticus Finch would do in Harper Lee's classic novel *To Kill A Mockingbird*. We can never tell what it is like until we walk in someone else's shoes. As patient and tolerant as Atticus was when an angry citizen spat on his face, we, in the healthcare profession, are called to the same standards.

 A VIRTUOUS HEALER WHO EXEMPLIFIED
PATIENCE, TOLERANCE AND UNDERSTANDING

Saint Thérèse of Lisieux (Sister Thérèse of the Child Jesus)
(1 8 7 3 – 1 8 9 7)

When Saint Thérèse died at the tender age of twenty-four, having spent ten years in the Carmelite convent of Lisieux, it is said that some of the nuns were quite concerned about what to write in her obituary. To those unaware of her mystical nature which she kept under wraps, she was just an ordinary cloistered nun. Thérèse did not hold an important position in the convent, except as unofficial novice mistress; some nuns were at a loss in describing her legacy, if any.

Yet, this obscure Carmelite nun had left a spiritual autobiography, entitled *Story of a Soul*. Sister Thérèse had written the book at the request of her prioress, her older sister Pauline. In it she described a simple spirituality she called "the little way." She wrote a kind of spiritual handbook that anyone—in or out of the monastery, educated or not, rich or poor,

young or old—could follow. Sister Thérèse said anyone can perform ordinary tasks, endure small hurts and trust God like a little child trusts her
parents. Through this pathway of spiritual childhood, anyone can hope
to attain holiness. In Saint Thérèse's own words:

> I've always desired to be a saint, but alas! ...when I've compared myself to the
> Saints...there is between them and me the same difference that exists
> between a mountain the summit of which is lost in the sky, and an obscure
> grain of sand that is trodden under foot by passersby. Instead of becoming
> discouraged, I've told myself: God wouldn't know how to inspire desires that
> can't be realized. So despite my littleness I can aspire to sainthood. To make
> myself bigger is impossible; I have to put up with myself such as I am with
> all my imperfections. But I want to seek the means of going to heaven by a
> little way that is very straight, very short, a completely new way.
>
> We're in an age of inventions. Now there's no more need to climb the
> steps of a staircase. In rich homes there are elevators…. I would also like to
> find an elevator to lift me up to Jesus, because I'm too little to climb the rough
> staircase of perfection. So I sought in the holy books the indication of the ele-
> vator…and I read these words…: "Let all who are *simple* come to my
> house"….
>
> The elevator that must lift me up to heaven is Your arms, Jesus! For that
> I don't need to become big. On the contrary, I have to stay little—may I
> become little, more and more.[1]

The *Story of a Soul*, which was published two years posthumously, quickly
became a phenomenal best-seller. It was translated from the original French
to English in 1901 and, in 1912, the first complete edition of the life of
Thérèse, the Little Flower, including "Letters and Spiritual Counsels" was
published. Soon thereafter, devotion to "the Little Flower" flourished.

Countless miracles were attributed to her intercession, true to the
promise she had made that after her death that she would "let fall a
shower of roses. I will spend my heaven in doing good upon earth."[2]
Declared a saint twenty-eight years after her death—an exceptionally
short period for beatification and canonization—Saint Thérèse of Lisieux

quickly became one of the most popular saints in the modern era. She is one of only three women in the history of the Catholic church, the others being Saint Teresa of Avila and Saint Catherine of Siena, who have been declared doctors of the church because of their invaluable theological contributions.

Though she never left the walls of her Carmelite convent, Sister Thérèse is venerated as the patron saint of missionaries because of her special love and keen admiration for missionary work, eloquently expressed through her prayers and letters.

Thérèse was born in Alençon, France on January 2, 1873, to Louis and Zélie Martin, a devout couple whose cause for beatification is in process. They had married with the intent of keeping a strict vow of celibacy, but a priest wisely advised Louis and Zélie that God would prefer if they started a family. They followed the advice to the letter, prolifically producing nine children, five of whom (Pauline, Marie, Leonie, Celine and Thérèse) entered religious life. One, of course, became a great saint!

Louis, a watchmaker, was an exceptionally loving husband and caring father. When Zélie succumbed to breast cancer, Thérèse was only four years old. Louis raised the children with help from his eldest daughter, sixteen-year-old Pauline. She assumed the role of mother to little Thérèse and, later, as Carmelite prioress, asked Thérèse to write an autobiography.

As a young child, Thérèse reportedly saw the Blessed Virgin Mary smile at her while she was praying in front of her statue together with her other sisters. She was sick at the time and the apparition instantly cured her of her illness. By age eleven, Thérèse had significantly advanced in her prayer life. She found a comfortable corner in her room where she would spend time in solitude and meditation.

Educated by the Benedictines and eager to follow in the footsteps of her sisters, fourteen-year-old Thérèse longed to enter the Carmelite convent in Lisieux. When the superior of the convent rejected her application citing her age, Thérèse approached the local bishop who also refused. Determined to enter religious life, particularly after her "conversion" on Christmas 1886, Thérèse traveled with her father and her sister Celine on a pilgrimage to Rome. They had an audience with Pope Leo XIII who listened to Thérèse's request. With the pontiff's blessing, she entered the convent of Lisieux on April 9, 1888, at the tender age of fifteen, happily joining her older sisters Pauline and Marie. Celine joined the convent after their father had passed away.

Thérèse took on ordinary duties with extraordinary joy. She was grateful for every little problem, every little inconvenience, every painful experience—these she considered "treasures" along her "easy" pathway toward sanctity. When she was irritated by a particularly annoying nun, she kept her temper in check and went out of her way to do special favors for her.

> ...I was doing laundry with a Sister who kept throwing dirty water in my face each time she picked up the handkerchiefs on her bench. My first movement was to draw back and dry my face, in order to show the Sister who was sprinkling me that she would do me a service if she would move gently, but immediately I thought that I was quite silly to refuse treasures that had been given to me so generously, and I took great care not to let my struggle show. I made every effort to desire to receive a lot of dirty water, so that in the end I had really taken a liking to this new form of sprinkling with holy water, and I promised myself to come back another time to that happy place where one received so many treasures.[3]

Reading these accounts, we might get the impression that Sister Thérèse was a somber and dull character. On the contrary, Sister Marie of the Angels, novice mistress at Lisieux, commenting on twenty-year-old Thérèse, wrote in 1893: "[Her] head is filled with tricks to be played on anyone she pleases. A mystic, a *comedienne*, she is everything! She can make you shed tears of devotion, and she can just as easily make you split your sides with laughter...."[4]

She was human, all right. Thérèse occasionally fell asleep while praying. But rather than worrying about it, she comforted herself with the thought that mothers love their children all the time, even when their children fall asleep in their arms. God, she reasoned, must love us even when we fall asleep in prayer.

As gentle and patient as she was, Thérèse was relentless in her pursuit of holiness.

> I feel within me the vocation of *Priest*…. But alas! While desiring to be a Priest, I admire and envy the humility of St. Francis of Assisi…in refusing the sublime dignity of the priesthood….
>
> I have the *vocation* to be an Apostle…. I would like to travel across the world…I would like to be a missionary…I would like to shed my blood for You….
>
> Martyrdom: That is the dream of my youth. That dream has grown within me….
>
> Charity gave me the key to my vocation. I understood that if the Church had a body composed of different members…, it was not missing the most necessary, the most noble of all: I understood that the Church had a heart, and that this heart was *burning with Love*…. I understood that *Love* contains all the Vocations, that Love is all, that it embraces all times and all places…in a word, that it is Everlasting!
>
> Then in the excess of my delirious joy, I cried out: Oh, Jesus, my Love…I have finally found my vocation: …My vocation is Love![5]

Thérèse woke up one morning, in 1896, with hemoptysis (coughing up blood). Even as her health deteriorated, she kept smiling and carried on her daily routines so that no one knew she was seriously ill. On September 30, 1897, at age twenty-four, Thérèse died in the convent of Lisieux of pulmonary tuberculosis. Canonized in 1925, barely three decades after her death, Saint Thérèse instantly became one of the most beloved and popular saints. On the hundredth anniversary of her death, her reliquary was viewed and venerated by millions as it was transported around the world.

QUESTIONS FOR REFLECTIONS

1. How many times did you lose your temper this week?
2. What pushed your buttons? A careless remark, misplaced lab or X-ray reports, delays in treatment, annoying interruptions, unnecessary inconveniences?
3. Did yelling and screaming change anything? Did blowing off steam make you feel better or worse?
4. When was the last time you apologized for getting angry?

SPIRITUAL EXERCISE

Say a prayer and ask God to bless the one person who hurt you most today. Better still, write a short letter of forgiveness. (You may or may not mail the letter.) Alternatively, write the person's name on a book of prayer found in most churches. Or simply light a candle for him or her.

PRAYER

Lord, make me an instrument of your peace.

Where there is hatred, let me sow love.

Where there is injury, pardon.

Where there is doubt, faith.

Where there is despair, hope.

Where there is darkness, light.

Where there is sadness, joy.

O, Divine Master, grant that I may not so much seek

To be consoled as to console,

to be understood as to understand,

to be loved as to love,

For it is in giving that we receive,

It is in pardoning that we are pardoned,

And it is in dying that we are born again to eternal life.

—Attributed to Saint Francis of Assisi[6]

notes

[1] Saint Thérèse of Lisieux, *The Story of a Soul: A New Translation*. Robert J. Edmonson, C.J., trans. and ed. (Brewster, Mass.: Paraclete, 2006), pp. 229–231.

[2] Quoted in Ellsberg, p. 429.

[3] Saint Thérèse of Lisieux, p. 285.

[4] *Saint Thérèse of Lisieux: Her Last Conversations*, John Clarke, O.C.D., trans. (Washington, D.C.: ICS, 1977), p. 16.

[5] Saint Thérèse of Lisieux, pp. 214–217.

[6] Gloria Hutchinson. *Six Ways to Pray from Six Great Saints* (Cincinnati: St. Anthony Messenger Press, 1982), p. 24.

four

SCRUBBING WITH PRAYER

Contemplation in Action

*"But whenever you pray, go into your room and shut the door and
pray to your Father who is in secret; and your Father who sees in
secret will reward you."*

—MATTHEW 6:6

I once belonged to a contemplative prayer group. We would gather daily
(which I often missed) or once a week at the monastery. Sister Mary
would open the monastery side door to welcome us at 5:30 AM and at
3:00 PM. Then she would lead us in a twenty-minute session of silent
(contemplative or centering) prayer.

We usually started the prayer session with a brief scriptural passage.
Once in a while, after the prayer session, Sister Mary would give us spiritual direction. More often than not, the subject would come around to
how we can pray daily, how we can carve time out of our busy lives to
spend private moments with God. That seemed to be the most difficult
problem for everyone in the group.

Whether a homemaker or a neurosurgeon, a research scientist or a real
estate broker, teacher or janitor, we all have our busy schedules. Pagers,
cell phones, Palm Pilots, laptops, e-mails, faxes—all these technological

wonders have become modern symbols of how our lives are packed full of activities. Or, if not with activities, with constant interruptions.

People in our prayer group (a nun, an auto mechanic, a social worker) talked about getting up at five in the morning, like the monks do, to pray the office of the hours (Vigils). Or we talked about retiring at night to a room or closet to pray Vespers or Compline.

I envy those who can pray Vigils/Lauds and Vespers/Compline with regularity, because I can't. I often work late into the night and miss Vespers, because I have to attend to emergency appendectomies or late-night car crashes. At times I go home to sleep at 3 or 4 AM just as the monks at Camaldoli or Prince of Peace are getting up to pray.

Frequently, I work all day at the clinic or run between hospitals and hardly have time to eat lunch, let alone time to spend fifteen or thirty minutes praying. When I started surgical residency, a wise old professor had cautioned us young surgeons to get used to eating once a day. We laughed at what we thought at that time was a lame joke. Well, thirty years later, I know better.

After trying several strategies (one monk told me I needed to approach my prayer life like a guerilla fighter—constantly looking for hidden opportunities), I have resorted to praying before an operation. A surgeon traditionally scrubbed for five to ten minutes before stepping into the operating theater and gowning for an operation. Now, with the availability of more potent antibacterial soap, sterilizing the hands and forearms can be done in seconds, but I try not follow this practice. One, because the newer bacterial solutions are not as gentle to my skin; and, two, because scrub time can be a valuable time for prayer. Some surgeons use the time they save prepping to plan for the operation. Like others, I use it to pray.

As I soak my hands and start a slow methodical scrub, I say a prayer for the patient, asking God to make the operation a success; for the patient's family, and parents, spouse and children, and friends, who are anxiously waiting for the operation to finish; I pray that the surgical team and I will perform the operation well; I pray that we be useful instruments of God's healing and grace.

It has been said that God wants to accomplish things in the world but, after the seven Biblical days of creation were done and over with, God has to wait for us to come around and willingly become instruments in the continuing work on earth.

It is a humbling thought.

VIRTUOUS HEALERS WHO EXEMPLIFIED CONTEMPLATION IN ACTION

Brother Lawrence
(1614–1691)

"The most holy practice, the nearest to daily life, and the most essential for the spiritual life, is the practice of the presence of God, that is to find joy in his divine company and to make it a habit of life, speaking humbly and conversing lovingly with him at all times, every moment, without rule or restriction, above all at times of temptation, distress, dryness, and revulsion, and even faithfulness and sin....

We should apply ourselves continually, so that, without exception, all our actions become small occasions of fellowship with God, yet artlessly..."[1]

—BROTHER LAWRENCE

It may surprise us that such wisdom is found in abundance in a tiny seventeenth-century book, *The Practice of the Presence of God*, written by a simple Carmelite layman, Brother Lawrence, who spent most of his life working in the kitchen of a monastery in Paris. Yet his wise counsel has grown in popularity through the centuries and indeed has helped many advance in the spiritual life.

Brother Lawrence was born Nicholas Herman in 1614 in Hériménil, near Lunéville, in the Lorraine district of France. Though intelligent, he achieved only an elementary education, as his parents could not afford to send him to higher education. As a young man, he enlisted in the army and was sent to the battlefield in the Thirty Years' War. He was captured and imprisoned but was later released. He sustained serious leg injuries in the battle of Rambervillers in 1635, from which he never fully recovered.

Back home, he consulted his uncle, Jean Majeur, a Discalced Carmelite, regarding his future plans. Thereafter, assisted by a friend, Nicholas built a hermitage. The project did not last long, however, and he went on to serve at the home of Monsieur de Freubet, a prominent banker in Paris.

In 1640, twenty-six-year-old Nicholas entered the Discalced Carmelite priory in Paris, as a lay brother. Lacking a formal education, particularly in Latin, he was not eligible for higher clerical orders. Nicholas made his solemn profession of vows in 1642 and assumed the religious name Brother Lawrence of the Resurrection. He spent the rest of his life toiling in the relative obscurity of the monastery kitchen. Except for two trips to purchase wine for the priory, in 1665 to Auvergne and in 1666 to Bourgogne, Brother Lawrence spent his entire adult life within the priory. In his senior years, as his health declined, Brother Lawrence was assigned the humbler task of repairing sandals for over a hundred friars, an assignment he joyfully carried out.

While his position in the priory was humble and lowly, Brother Lawrence gradually gained recognition as a great spiritual director. Religious and laity alike, both near and far from the monastery, sought him for spiritual direction. Father Joseph de Beaufort, one of his directees, compiled notes of his conversations with Brother Lawrence and collected letters of direction and other maxims. His editorial work produced the spiritual classic, *The Practice of the Presence of God.*

Brother Lawrence's spirituality at first reading appears simple, yet (like Saint Thérèse's) is replete with practical theological insight and wisdom. In whatever circumstance we find ourselves, whatever task we do, whether great or small, important or insignificant, in the final analysis does not matter, if we perform the task in God's loving presence. In this context, there is no difference among scrubbing before surgery, performing the operation, talking to a patient's family or spending time in the chapel. For a homemaker, for instance, there is no difference among washing the dishes, picking up the kids from school, attending a Bible meeting or spending the night in prayerful contemplation.

Such practical spirituality makes sanctity accessible to everyone, whatever their state in life may be. It places holiness in the hands of a busy nurse as well as in the hands of a paralyzed, bedridden patient. Such teaching opens heaven's gate to the pope and to the pauper. It allows everyone, no matter the circumstances to fulfill the scriptural advice to pray without ceasing. Brother Lawrence offers the most simple prescription for an accessible prayer life, "We should apply ourselves continually, so that, without exception, all our actions become small occasions of fellowship with God."[2]

While Brother Lawrence's spirituality may sound simple, he cautioned his directees that achieving awareness of God's presence required diligent effort, at least at the beginning.

Brother Lawrence also had some interesting things to say about health and sickness. It is helpful to bear in mind that seventeenth-century medicine was embryonic and doctors were more often than not summoned to the bedside when patients were literally at death's door. Yet, Brother Lawrence's advice to trust God rather than physicians may be relevant to our times particularly since we now put so much reliance on science and technology:

I wish you could believe that God is often nearer to us in our times of sickness and infirmity, than when we are enjoying perfect health. Seek no other medicine than him. To the best of my understanding, he wishes to heal us alone. Put all your trust in him. You will soon see the results.[3]

From a place as humble as a monastery kitchen, doing ordinary things such as peeling potatoes and boiling soup, Brother Lawrence touched the lives of many and, through his tiny book, has continued to do so through the ages. Brother Lawrence of the Resurrection died at age seventy-seven on February 12, 1691.

Saint John of God

(1 4 9 5 – 1 5 5 0)

John was born in Montemoro Novo, Evora, Portugal, on March 8, 1495. At age eight, he left home to assist a mendicant priest, wandering homeless in the kingdom of Castile in Spain. At age twenty-two, he enlisted in the army of Charles V. He was captured in the Spanish war against France and kept as prisoner of war. Dissatisfied with a life that was at best aimless, he left the military (actually, an account says he was thrown out after being stripped and flagellated) and, on a whim, embarked on a pilgrimage to Santiago de Compostela, which led to his conversion.

Resolving to lead a reformed life at age thirty-eight, he went back home only to discover that his parents had died in his absence. Deeply saddened, he impulsively decided to become a missionary and prepared to travel to North Africa to set Christian slaves free by taking their place and perhaps to undergo martyrdom. But John was persuaded by his confessor to abandon the hasty plan. Instead, he began selling holy cards, novenas, religious items and spiritual books around the towns and villages of Gibraltar. Later, he opened a religious store in Granada. After a brief stay in the psychiatric ward at the Royal Hospital for what turned out to be a misdiagnosis (he had beaten himself in public, loudly lamenting his past sins and tore his clothes off), he started a shelter for the poor and the homeless. He roamed the city streets of Granada looking for patients, carrying those unable to walk on his shoulders. His shelter grew into a small hospital, located in an old Carmelite monastery. He took care of the sick, the dying, the disabled, outcasts, alcoholics, ex-convicts, prostitutes and derelicts. Without asking questions or screening for potential criminals, he took in anyone and everyone who needed care, food and a warm bed. This caused an uproar; but, John assured the town folk that there was no sinner worse than himself.

He financed his hospital with donations and by selling books and firewood in the public square. As his work became known, the local archbishop approved of his mission, gave him a religious habit and called him John of God. The town's leaders, including the Marquis of Tarifa, asked John to manage the local hospital. Volunteers, including priests, physicians and nurses, helped John staff the charity hospital.

John's tremendous ministry was sustained by personal prayer, contemplation and mortification. He was known to be blessed with mystical visions. Once, he was tending to a beggar, washing his feet, when the man was transfigured, engulfing John in so radiant a light that witnesses thought he was ablaze. At another time he heard Jesus say: "John, all you do for the poor in my name is done for me. It is my hand that receives your alms; it is my body that you clothe, my feet that you wash."[4]

One famous miracle related to John of God occurred during a fire which engulfed the Royal Hospital at Granada. After rescuing trapped patients, John returned to the building to save anything he could, throwing mattresses and blankets out of the window. He fell through the burning floor. People thought he had plunged to his death, but the saint miraculously emerged from the flames unharmed. Thus, John of God became one of the patron saints of firefighters, though Saint Florian is the more popular and well-known patron of firefighters.

John died from complications of pneumonia, incurred after trying to save a drowning victim, in Granada, on March 8, 1550, at age fifty-five. His medical missionary work was officially recognized by the church in 1571 as the Order of the Brothers Hospitallers. Presently, the religious order is actively ministering in forty-nine countries around the world. John of God was beatified by Pope Urban VIII in 1638 and canonized by Pope Alexander VIII in 1690. He was declared patron saint of hospitals, nurses, cardiac patients and the dying. He is also the patron saint of booksellers, publishers and printers.

QUESTIONS FOR REFLECTION

1. How often each day do you pray?
2. Is it difficult for you to talk to God every day? Why?
3. In lieu of asking God for favors, can you simply sit down and listen?

SPIRITUAL EXERCISE

Sit in a comfortable chair. Close your eyes. Take a deep breath...and another one.

Put your hands together. Relax.... Place yourself gently in God's presence. Enjoy.

PRAYER

Lord, teach me to pray.

notes

[1] Brother Lawrence, *The Practice of the Presence of God: Based on the Conversations, Letters, Ways and Spiritual Principles of Brother Lawrence, as well as on the writings of Joseph De Beaufort*, E.M. Blaiklock, trans. (New York: Thomas Nelson, 1981), p. 68.

[2] Brother Lawrence, p. 68.

[3] Brother Lawrence, p. 54.

[4] Ellsberg, p. 108.

f i v e

TAKING A STANCE
Courage and Fortitude

"Very truly, I tell you, unless a grain of wheat falls into the earth and dies, it remains just a single grain; but if it dies, it bears much fruit."

—JOHN 12:24

Not so long ago, physicians carried everything they needed in their medicine bags—penicillin, syringes, needles, tongue depressors, a stethoscope, an otoscope and a prescription pad. My father-in-law was one of those old-timers. The technology was "backward" compared to what we have today, a constantly evolving checklist of spiral CTs, MRIs, cardiac caths, portable sonograms, telemetry, cell savers, endoscopes, harmonic scalpels, digital laparoscopes, robots, telemedicine. Medicine was admittedly "primitive" in the not-so-distant past. But the mission was clear: alleviate suffering, treat the sick, save lives.

It was simpler in the old days—or so it seems. By and large, hospitals were built by religious communities to care for the sick. The original hospitals also provided shelter to the homeless and food for the hungry. In medieval times, hospitals served as welcoming stations for travelers and pilgrims, thus the old French term for *hospital* was *hotel-Dieu* or "hostel of God."

The link between religion and medicine may be traced as far back as ancient Egypt and Greece when temples of worship served as rudimentary hospitals. In 325, the First Council of Nicaea officially provided care for the poor and the sick by ordering the construction of a hospital in every town with a cathedral. Thus was built the hospital in Constantinople under the direction of Saint Sampson, the physician.

Times have changed. Now it's the money, not the mission. Profit rather than charity. The type of medicine practiced today in the United States has morphed into a financial Frankenstein of sorts, a creature driven by managed care and bureaucratic directives.

When a healthcare service is proposed for the benefit of the community, for instance, the reaction is often along the lines of: What is the bottom line? Will it be profitable for the hospital? Who will reap the profits? Little attention, if any, is given to: How will such a service benefit the people in our community? The critical question no longer is: How will this service or program impact the health of our patients? The new criterion is: How much money will this program generate?

The increasingly capitalistic philosophy which has captivated modern medicine is justified by the assumption that unless financial factors are given primary consideration, the hospital or health establishment will run out of funds to carry on its mission. There is truth in that assumption. However, the pendulum has swung too far to the side of the money changers and bean counters. Consequently, primary caregivers, in their role as patient advocates, find themselves increasingly at odds with insurance carriers, HMO reviewers, government entities and hospital administration. In the tug-of-war between mission and medicine, patients often lose.

People treating and caring for the sick are rarely political creatures. In the course of protracted conflicts involving approval and funding of necessary treatments, physicians, nurses and other healthcare professionals who vigorously advocate for their patients burn out. We eventually either join the other side in the money venture (by forming our own for-profit organizations) or become cynical and bail out. In either case, we begin to lose the courage of our convictions and, unknowingly, sell our souls.

VIRTUOUS HEALERS WHO EXEMPLIFIED COURAGE AND FORTITUDE

Saint Maximilian Kolbe
(1894–1941)

Father Maximilian Kolbe courageously took a stance and paid the ultimate price for his convictions. Raymond Kolbe was born in Zdunska Wola, Poland, on January 8, 1894. He entered the Conventual Franciscan Order, adopting the name Maximilian, when he was sixteen years old. Later, he pursued further education in Rome, and was ordained to the priesthood at age twenty-four.

To promote devotion to the Blessed Virgin Mary, Father Maximilian Kolbe founded the Immaculata movement in 1927. He successfully launched several publications including a daily paper and a magazine, *The Knight of the Immaculata*, which reputedly enjoyed a circulation of over one million. He also helped organize a community of about eight hundred friars, the largest men's religious community in the world.

Father Kolbe traveled to Japan and India, spreading the Immaculata movement with remarkable zeal. Afflicted with tuberculosis, he returned to Poland in 1936 to recuperate. Three years later, when the Germans invaded, his monastery was ransacked and he was imprisoned with forty other friars. Father Kolbe was released three months later but, on February 17, 1941, was arrested again, charged with sheltering and feeding thousands of refugee Jews and Poles.

On May 28, 1941, Father Maximilian was sent to the concentration camp at Auschwitz. Ordered to wear a convict's garb and tattooed with the number 16670, Father Maximilian was assigned to heavy labor, hauling stone blocks for a crematorium.

On the night of August 3, 1941 an inmate escaped from Maximilian's prison section. Consequently, "Butcher" Fritsch, the Nazi commandant, mandated that ten inmates, picked at random from the section, be starved to death. Sergeant Franciszek Gajowniek, among the unfortunate men marked for execution, broke down and cried, desperate that he would never see his family again. Touched by the young father's plea, Father Kolbe stepped forward and volunteered to take Sergeant Gajowniek's place. Asked why he was putting his life on the line, Father Kolbe replied: "I am a Catholic priest. I wish to die for that man. I am old, he has a wife and children." The commandant brusquely accepted Father Kolbe's offer, sparing Gajowniek's life.[1]

Confined to his death bunker, cell 18, to die by starvation, Father Kolbe attended to and spiritually nourished his nine starving companions. "The Nazis will not kill our souls," he comforted them. On August 14, 1941, Father Kolbe and three remaining survivors were administered lethal injections of carbolic acid[2] and cremated in the infamous ovens of Auschwitz.[3]

Pope Paul VI declared Father Maximilian Mary Kolbe blessed on October 17, 1971. Pope John Paul II canonized and proclaimed him a "martyr of charity" on October 10, 1982. The Gajowniek family attended the canonization ceremony.

Devotion to Saint Maximilian Kolbe is encouraged among families, the pro-life movement, journalists, prisoners and the chemically addicted.

Archbishop Oscar Arnulfo Romero

(1917–1980)

"A church that does not unite itself to the poor in order to denounce from the place of the poor the injustice committed against them is not truly the Church of Jesus Christ."[4]

—OSCAR ROMERO

Oscar Arnulfo Romero taught us by example what courage in our times can be. His transformation from conservative cleric to champion of liberation theology is worthy of our study and admiration.

Father Oscar Romero's appointment as archbishop in 1977 was welcome news to government officials who wanted a meek and conservative priest, someone they could control, to lead the church in El Salvador. To friend and foe alike, Father Romero was a safe choice; he was politically neutral and not identified with the ranks of liberation theologians. The respected prelate would not be a thorn in the government's side.

Indeed, as we read the story of this modern saint, or learn from the biographical film produced by the Paulist fathers, Archbishop Oscar Romero did not venture outside of traditional ecclesiastical circles. He was not a firebrand; he was a simple priest who loved the church and who loved to read.

Yet Archbishop Romero was not unaware of the social, economic and political conditions in El Salvador. Nor was he ill-informed regarding the Second Vatican Council's teachings on the preferential option for the poor. He was, in fact, a scholarly prelate who was acutely aware of the dehumanizing effect of his government's repressive policies. He spoke against its injustices soon after being installed archbishop of San Salvador. His weekly homilies, broadcast throughout the country, exposed and publicized the government's continuing violation of human rights. Applying Christ's teachings and scriptural references to the political situation in El Salvador, Archbishop Romero rose to become his nation's conscience.

The turning point in Archbishop Romero's public life came when activist Father Rutilio Grande, s.j., and his companions were ambushed and killed by government agents. In response to the tragedy, Archbishop Romero cancelled all Sunday Masses throughout El Salvador. He then invited the faithful to come to the main cathedral where he presided over the Requiem Mass held in memory of the beloved martyrs. Tens of thousands of Salvadorans attended the historic event and listened to their bishop's homily:

> I rejoice, brothers and sisters, that our church is persecuted precisely for its preferential option for the poor and for seeking to become incarnate in the interests of the poor.... How sad it would be in a country where such horrible murders are being committed if there were no priests among the victims.[5]

At risk of alienating friends and family who were an integral part of the Salvadoran oligarchy, and of enduring criticism from his fellow bishops who ironically were sympathetic to the dictatorship, Archbishop Romero pressed on in his crusade for peace and social justice. He suffered much by taking this stance.

While celebrating Mass on March 24, 1980, in the chapel of the Carmelite hospital where he resided, Archbishop Romero was shot and killed by hired assassins. He was the first bishop murdered on the altar since Thomas Becket eight centuries earlier.

Two weeks before his assassination, Archbishop Romero had said: "[A]s a Christian, I do not believe in death without resurrection. If I am killed, I shall arise in the Salvadoran people.... A bishop will die, but God's church, which is the people, will never perish."[6]

QUESTIONS FOR REFLECTION

1. Do you have the courage to seek the truth and to stand by it to the end despite the risk of compromising your career, your future?

2. Do you think you would be able to do what Father Maximilian Kolbe and Archbishop Romero did—lay down your life for another or for justice?

SPIRITUAL EXERCISE

Make a list of things you think must change.

How can you change them?

If you cannot change them, what can you do to change how you react to them?

PRAYER

Lord, grant me the serenity to accept
the things I cannot change,
the courage to change the things that I can,
and the wisdom to know the difference.

notes

[1] The Secular Franciscan Home Page, http://secularfranciscans.org.

[2] Ironically, carbolic acid merits a special place in the history of medicine and surgery. In the 1860s, Joseph Lister pioneered the use of carbolic acid as a cleansing agent and disinfectant. Prior to Lister's discovery of antisepsis, approximately 80 percent of surgical patients developed infection and gangrene.

[3] Ellsberg, p. 35.

[4] Ellsberg, p. 132.

[5] Ellsberg, p. 131.

[6] James R. Brockman. *Romero: A Life* (Maryknoll, N.Y.: Orbis, 1989), p. 248.

six

FRODO'S RING

Humility and Temperance

"The greatest among you will be your servant. All who exalt themselves will be humbled, and all who humble themselves will be exalted."

— MATTHEW 23:11–12

"Whoever wants to be first must be last of all and servant of all."

— MARK 9:35

We're putting the final stitches in the Gore-Tex graft, repairing the ruptured aortic aneurysm. The seventy-six-year-old retired barber had practically bled to death on the operating table. To top it off, his heart had stopped for a full minute before we shocked it back to sinus rhythm. Yet we could not be certain if restricted blood flow to the brain when his heart had stopped had damaged critical areas of the brain. The EKG monitor documented a full minute when his heart was not pumping (asystole) but it was likely his stressed heart had been failing to deliver sufficient blood (and nutrition) to the brain much earlier. Already his Foley bag showed he was not making enough urine, indicating that blood flow to the kidneys had been compromised.

"Ours is a humbling profession," my co-surgeon remarked. I nodded in agreement. It had taken three hours of intense focus, concentration and teamwork to stop the hemorrhage from the largest artery in the body. True, we had saved a man's life—but were our efforts good enough to bring him back to full recovery? His kidneys might recover but could we successfully get him off the ventilator and would he eventually emerge from the coma?

Medicine is a humbling profession. Yet, does practicing it make us humble men and women? Do patients regard us individually and as a class of people as genuinely humble?

It's not surprising that most people consider doctors to be more privileged and proud than deprived and humble. And we surgeons don't help this misperception by often displaying type-A aggressive personalities.

There was a time in our lives when we thought we had it all. It could have been when we got out of medical school, or when we passed the licensing board or the specialty certification exam when it seemed there was little, if anything, in medicine we did not know. Yet as we gained more experience and knowledge, we quickly realized how much more there was to learn.

I remember my father telling me that medicine, like law (he was a lawyer), was a lifelong study. And that the textbooks we read in school were merely the foundation of more learning to come. In my naiveté, I thought he meant continuing medical education courses and updates. And while he did mean these, he also implied more. I came to understand the wisdom in his remark twenty years later, as it echoed in the remarks of a senior surgeon. The wise old professor felt like a good surgeon, he said, when he had successfully finished a complicated case in the OR. However, he felt he had truly become a physician—partaker of a noble tradition and a true disciple of Hippocrates—when he comforted dying patients and grieving families.

Many years back, when I was in medical academia, many of us seemed to revel (at least on Saturday morning grand rounds) in besting each other, in the quickness with which we quoted the latest surgical study, in arriving at the correct diagnosis faster than anyone else. To a certain extent, the university environment and prevailing culture nurtured in young physicians and medical students an arrogant attitude, afflicting them with the so-called "ivory tower syndrome" rather than inculcating in them a sense that they were to become humble members and judicious bearers of a noble tradition and profession.

Perhaps, the goal of encouraging mental quickness and confidence is laudable. Yet why don't many senior physicians look back fondly at their residency years? Many in fact view those years of training with contempt, frequently referring to that period of their lives as their "passage through slavery."

In an effort to instill confidence and trust in our patients, we often need to show that we are in full control of the situation, that we know exactly how tomorrow will unfold. Patients and their families, shaken by the illness that has injected uncertainty into their lives, look to us for assurance, laying their doubts and fears in our hands. Yet, how often we are surprised by clinical findings we did not anticipate, pathology we did not expect, results we did not foresee.

We think it's a routine case of appendicitis, and it turns out to be Crohn's disease. We think stones in the bile ducts and it's cholangiocarcinoma (cancer of the bile duct). We think splenic laceration and it's a splenic artery aneurysm. Pulmonary contusion (bruising of the lungs) and it's injury to the superior vena cava.

Despite groundbreaking technological advances (spiral CT scans, MRIs, angiograms, endoscopes), studies show that a postmortem will change the clinical diagnosis by as much as forty to sixty percent. In other words, despite modern imaging capabilities which have magnified our ability to visualize the human body and uncover its minutest secrets, we still miss many diseases. On the other hand, insurance carriers, government agencies and trial lawyers, expect doctors to be correct 100 percent of the time.

One might compare the art and science of medicine to Frodo's ring in J.R.R. Tolkien's classic *The Lord of the Rings*. To the bearer, the powerful ring conferred a privilege and imposed a burden. It also directed the bearer's heart either toward pride or toward humility.

 VIRTUOUS HEALERS WHO EXEMPLIFIED
HUMILITY AND TEMPERANCE

Blessed Charles de Foucauld

(1 8 5 8 – 1 9 1 6)

Viscount Charles Eugene de Foucauld was born into an aristocratic family in Strasbourg, France, on September 15, 1858. He was orphaned at age five and grew up with his sister, Maria, and with cousin Marie Moitessier, whose spirituality became an important influence in his life.

The beneficiary of a substantial inheritance, Charles enrolled at Saint-Cyr Military Academy to please his maternal grandfather, a retired colonel, and at the cavalry school in Saumur, barely managing to graduate in 1879, ranked eighty-sixth in a class of eighty-seven. School records noted that Charles was "a remarkable person…with no thought for anything except entertainment."[1] After graduation, he was commissioned as second lieutenant in the French army contingent in Algeria. However, his rebelliousness and cavalier relationship with an attractive young lady irked his superiors, forcing him to leave the garrison of Pont-a-Mousson in 1881. He redeemed himself militarily during an ensuing revolt in the Sahara and his rank was restored. Disgusted with military life, he eventually resigned from the army.

Unencumbered by commitments, he left for an expedition in the Sahara to map the region along Morocco's Algerian border. To gain passage across the border, Charles joined a caravan of Eastern European and Middle Eastern Jews. Fluent in foreign languages, he assumed the identity of a Russian rabbi's servant.

Upon his return to Paris, he published his topographical, ethnic and social findings as *Reconnaissance au Maroc, 1883–1884*, which was well received by the Geographical Society of Paris. He then geared up for a second expedition (1885–1886), to map the oases in southern Algeria and Tunisia. During these explorations, Charles learned the mores and customs of nomadic tribes and was troubled by their intertribal conflicts and inhuman practice of slavery.

In 1886, Charles spent time with Marie Moitessier in Paris as he finalized his presentations on Saharan topography. An agnostic, Charles nevertheless enjoyed their discussions on faith and religion. Soon, Marie introduced Charles to her confessor, Abbé Henri Huvelin, a diocesan priest. Tentatively taking the first steps of a spiritual expedition, Charles began visiting several churches, praying: "My God, if you exist, make your existence known to me."[2]

One day in October 1886, Charles sought Abbé Huvelin at the church of Saint Augustine for spiritual direction. The priest suggested that Charles embark on his religious quest with a general confession. The abundance of grace he received in the sacrament of reconciliation led to his radical conversion. Charles would later remark, "My religious vocation dates from the same hour as my faith: God is so great."[3]

In 1890, Charles entered the Trappist Abbey of Our Lady of the Snows. Three significant influences had converged to solidify his religious vocation: First, Abbé Huvelin's sermon relating to Christ's preference for the last place. Second, the image of a Trappist monk, clothed in a tattered habit, appearing like a beggar. Third, a pilgrimage to the Holy

Land where he encountered the hidden life of Jesus, totally devoid of prestige, power and privilege. Henceforth, Charles resolved to always take the last place, to appear like a beggar and to live a hidden, simple life in imitation of Jesus Christ.

From Our Lady of the Snows, Charles moved to a poorer monastery in Syria. There he dreamed of forming a simple religious community. He drafted a rule for a small community and sent it to Abbé Huvelin for his comments. The priest wrote back: "Live as a poor person…as abjectly as you like, but I beg of you, don't write a rule for others."[4]

His superiors wanted him to become a priest but, seeking a more solitary life of prayer and extreme poverty, Charles departed from Syria in 1897 to become a hermit, living as a servant in the convent of the Poor Clares in Nazareth. He ran errands for the congregation and worked as a handyman. Every day, he set aside time for prayer, writing a journal, reading and studying Scripture. It was said that he prayed all night in the chapel in adoration of the Blessed Sacrament. It was during such nocturnal adorations that he was called to become a missionary priest.

On June 9, 1901, Charles de Foucauld was ordained to the priesthood. He returned to Algeria and lived near a French military base. Eventually, he settled at Tamanrasset in the southern part of the Sahara, to live a hidden life in a harsh desert where temperatures could soar up to 120 degrees at midday and plunge to freezing at night. He learned the local language and prepared the first dictionary and grammar of the Touareg language. Known as Berberologues, the dictionary was published posthumously in four volumes. He also translated the four Gospels and some of the region's native poetry into Touareg.

The local tribes admired and respected the missionary hermit's life of poverty, prayer and hospitality. Father Charles did not preach to them because, "It would make as much sense to start by preaching the news of

Jesus to the Muslims here as it would for a Muslim preacher to go to a [Catholic] town in Brittany."[5]

Father Charles envisioned starting a simple religious order, stating,

> We wish to found…a small, humble hermitage where a few poor monks live on a little fruit and barley harvested with their own hands. They would live in a small, narrow enclosure in the penitence and adoration of the Holy Sacrament, never leaving and never preaching, but giving hospitality to anyone who comes, good or bad, friend or enemy, Moslem or Christian…sharing the last crust of bread with every pauper, every guest, every stranger who comes and receiving every human being as a beloved brother.[6]

Regretfully, his dream did not materialize during his lifetime. On December 1, 1916, Father Charles de Foucauld was killed by a band of rioters during an anti-French uprising. A few years after his death, however, his life and writings became an inspiration to many. In 1933, groups of Christians formed themselves into fraternities, living incognito amongst the poor, sharing their experiences. They supported themselves financially by taking ordinary, low-paying jobs. Calling themselves the Little Brothers of Jesus, they did not preach nor teach Christianity but simply lived it. In 1939, dedicated Christian women, following de Foucauld's charism, also formed sororities, naming themselves the Little Sisters of Jesus.

Today, throughout the world, there are some nineteen different movements consisting of laity, priests and religious following Foucauld's charism by living incognito among the poor, taking on humble tasks like their neighbors and expressing their Christianity not by word but by simple deeds. An association of diocesan priests modeled after Charles de Foucauld is called Jesus Caritas. Father Charles de Foucauld was beatified by Pope Benedict XVI on November 13, 2005, at St. Peter's Basilica. Welcoming the pilgrims who gathered for the liturgy, including Touaregs from the Sahara, and speaking in French, Pope Benedict XVI reminded the faithful that Blessed Charles de Foucauld:

> In his contemplative and hidden life in Nazareth, he discovered the truth about the humanity of Jesus and invites us to contemplate the mystery of the Incarnation....
>
> He discovered that Jesus, who came to join us in our humanity, invites us to universal brotherhood...
>
> As a priest, placed the Eucharist and the Gospel at the heart of his life...[7]

Blessed Marianne Cope

(1838–1918)

For almost a century, Mother Marianne Cope's missionary work was overshadowed by the legendary fame of her missionary partner, Blessed Damien of Molokai. Her beatification on May 14, 2005, at St. Peter's Basilica by the newly elected Pope Benedict XVI finally brought recognition to the accomplishments of this remarkable American nun.

Marianne was born to Peter and Barbara Cope on January 23, 1838, in Hessen-Darmstadt, Germany. In 1840, the Copes immigrated to the United States and settled with their five children in Utica, New York. Completing her education, Marianne worked briefly in a factory until August 1862 when, at age twenty-four, she joined the Sisters of the Third Order of Saint Francis, in Syracuse, New York. She was eventually elected mother superior and became administrator of St. Joseph's Hospital in Syracuse.

In 1883, on the invitation of the bishop of Honolulu, Sister Marianne assembled a contingent of six Franciscan nuns and traveled to Hawaii to assist in the care of leprosy patients. Her missionary group operated the Kakaako Receiving Station near Honolulu, attending to patients with Hansen's disease before they were transported to the island of Molokai for quarantine. On the neighboring island of Maui, Sister Marianne opened a hospital and started a school for girls.

Sister Marianne volunteered to assist Father Damien de Veuster in running the leprosarium on Molokai. Initially, she focused her efforts toward the care of young girls and women afflicted with leprosy. After the death of Father Damien in 1899, Sister Marianne took over the operation of the men's leprosarium as well, thereby overseeing the care of all leprosy patients quarantined on the island of Molokai.

Mother Marianne, as she was later called, was known for the very high standards she set for nursing care. For instance, she insisted on strict hygiene for all levels of caregivers—whether physicians, nurses or volunteers. Thus, no one under her supervision got infected with Hansen's disease, despite close and almost daily contact with leprosy patients. Despite her many administrative tasks and demanding nursing duties, Mother Marianne found time to sew clothes for patients, play the piano for them and take them out on picnics.

Mother Marianne Cope died on the island of Molokai on August 9, 1918, at the age of eighty, having spent thirty-five years of her remarkable life tirelessly serving lepers in Hawaii.

QUESTIONS FOR REFLECTION

1. Someone said that when you become aware of your humility, you've lost it. Have you ever experienced a time when you felt you were being humble, but weren't?

2. Do you ever feel like you are "too good" for something? That you are "entitled" to something more out of life? Why do you feel this way? Do you think your feelings are justified?

SPIRITUAL EXERCISE

Following the little way of Saint Thérèse, the Little Flower, recall someone who recently insulted you or said some bad things about you. Say a prayer for that person. If in church, light a candle for that individual. Realize the innate goodness of your fellow human being. He or she is no less a child of God—with shortcomings, perhaps, but who's perfect? Recall when you said some unkind things about others.

PRAYER

Prayer of the Little Brothers and Sisters of Jesus

O God, whose blessed Son became poor that we through his poverty might be rich: Deliver us from an inordinate love of this world, that we, inspired by the devotion of your servant Charles and those who have sought to carry on his work, may serve you with singleness of heart, and attain to the riches of the age to come; through Jesus Christ our Lord, who liveth and reigneth with thee, in the unity of the Holy Spirit, one God, now and forever.

notes

[1] Quoted in Charles de Foucauld, *Charles de Foucauld, Robert Ellsberg,* ed. and intro. (Maryknoll, N.Y.: Orbis, 1999), p. 16.

[2] Foucauld, p. 18.

[3] Kate White. The hidden life of Charles de Foucauld, *National Catholic Reporter,* November 11, 2005, available at www.ncronline.org.

[4] White.

[5] White.

[6] Foucauld, pp. 72–73.

[7] Address of Pope Benedict XVI, November 13, 2005. Available at www.vatican.va.

seven

KEEPING CODE BLUE GOING
Initiative, Discipline, Responsibility and Leadership

"If any want to become my followers, let them deny themselves and take up their cross and follow me."

—MARK 8:34

We are familiar with that dreadful moment. Thirty, forty-five minutes into the drill, we realize that the patient is slipping away. The spikes on the EKG monitor become irregular…the gaps between heartbeats widen…it's harder to sustain the blood pressure…the patient's skin is pale, cold, clammy….

We know we've crossed the threshold. The patient is not coming back. Yet, we keep on pumping the chest, pushing epinephrine, squeezing the breathing bag…desperately trying, hoping the vital signs will turn around and the patient will survive.

Physicians and nurses hardly give up on resuscitating critically ill patients. Even when survival looks dire, we "keep the code going." Yet, collectively, it seems we have given up on the struggle to revive the profession of medicine and nursing.

Like marathon runners, we pride ourselves in being disciplined, focused, persevering and tough. The fact that we survived medical and nursing school, countless hours in the classroom and in the lab, clerkship, internship, exam after exam, is a testament to our mettle. Yet, many of us, it seems, have given up the fight to keep healthcare alive.

Our clinical decisions have long been usurped by third-party payers, insurance clerks, discharge planners, claims adjustors and legions of bureaucrats. Other entities, far removed from clinical experience but armed with computer-generated data, now dictate which patients require hospitalization and which do not, what medicines to use and not to use for our patients, whether a CT scan or an MRI is appropriate, when patients can be discharged from the hospital, and which facility can provide appropriate care.

We studied long and hard so we could make accurate diagnoses and determine the right treatment for our patients. Yet, we are no longer skippers of the medical ship. In the name of cost-cutting, extraneous forces have pirated the ship and charted a new course for healthcare. If we are aboard at all, we have been relegated to being mere passengers, if not slaves, rowing and toiling blindly in the belly of the ship over whose direction we no longer have any control.

How can we extricate medicine and nursing from this morass? How can we steer the ship toward the right course? When will doctors and nurses, rather than politicians, bureaucrats and bean counters, take charge and run medicine again?

VIRTUOUS HEALERS WHO EXEMPLIFIED
INITIATIVE, DISCIPLINE, RESPONSIBILITY AND LEADERSHIP

Doctor Albert Schweitzer

(1 8 7 5 – 1 9 6 5)

Albert Schweitzer was born on January 14, 1875, in Alsace, along the border between France and Germany, into a family of ministers, musicians and scholars. An accomplished pianist and organist, his contribution to music extended to writing a biography on Johann Sebastian Bach in French, rewriting the book in German, and writing a book on organ building and playing.

He earned a doctorate in philosophy in 1899 at the University of Strasbourg and also studied at the Sorbonne and the University of Berlin. In 1900, he received a licentiate in theology and was appointed to the pastoral staff of St. Nicholai Church in Strasbourg. He later joined the philosophy and theology faculty at the University of Strasbourg and published several books on theology, the most important being *The Quest for the Historical Jesus* which established his reputation as a theological scholar.

His missionary spirit was awakened in 1904 upon reading an article in the Paris Missionary Society magazine appealing for physicians to volunteer in the French colony of Gabon. Convinced of the necessity for predominantly white Christian nations to atone for injustices imposed on black African people, he spoke to his congregation the following Sunday and said,

> We must make atonement for all the terrible crimes we read of in the newspapers. We must make atonement for the still worse ones, which we do not read about in the papers, crimes that are shrouded in the silence of the jungle night.[1]

Elaborating on the subject of racial injustice, he wrote that society's institutions had failed because of "the spirit of barbarism" which denied giving to all men "a human value and a human dignity." He decried the fact that "many sections of the human race have become merely raw material and property in human form."[2]

On October 13, 1905, writing to family and friends, he informed them of his decision to enter medical school so he could serve as a missionary physician in Africa. In contrast to music, philosophy or theology, the practice of medicine would, he explained, give him the opportunity "to work with my hands…. For years I have been giving myself out in words but this new form of activity would not be merely talking about the religion of love, but actually putting it into practice."[3]

His academic peers were surprised. Many of his friends said it was a big mistake to abandon a promising academic career. His family was concerned that he would waste his talents and languish in the African jungle. Some suggested he should use his influence instead to lecture on the need for medical assistance in Africa. Only Helene Bresslau, who later became his wife, stood by his decision.

Albert Schweitzer enrolled at the University of Strasbourg in 1905, and received a medical degree, with specialization in tropical medicine and surgery, at the age of thirty-eight. Ironically, the Paris Missionary Society for which he had radically reoriented his career, dedicating eight years of advanced education and training, rejected him! The Society was wary of physicians with theological backgrounds who might act too independently and become problematic for the society.

Undeterred, Doctor Schweitzer and his wife, Helene, a trained nurse by then, rallied friends for support. They raised sufficient funds to finance a hospital project in Africa for two years and offered the Paris Missionary Society a new proposal. Doctor Schweitzer would volunteer his medical services, pledging to "avoid everything that could cause offense to the missionaries and their converts in their belief."[4] After much discussion, the society accepted Doctor Schweitzer's offer but a key committee member resigned in protest.

Doctor Schweitzer and his wife left for the African continent in March 1913 and started their medical mission in a makeshift facility converted from a chicken coop. Soon, the project flourished and new buildings were constructed as the number of patients quickly increased.

When World War I broke out, Albert and Helene, being German citizens, were branded enemy aliens in the French Congo, and were deported as prisoners of war to St. Remy. Released from prison camp in 1918, the Schweitzers returned to their home in Alsace where they were blessed with the birth of their daughter Rhena.

Doctor Schweitzer spent the postwar years in Europe, delivering sermons and lectures, performing in concerts and writing *On the Edge of the Primeval Forest: The Decay and Restoration of Civilization, Civilization and Ethics* and *Christianity and the Religions of the World.* In 1920, while lecturing in Sweden, he described the concept of "Reverence for Life" as the universal principle of ethics, an idea he had conceived five years earlier:

> There flashed upon my mind the phrase Reverence for Life…. Man's ethics must not end with man, but should extend to the universe. He must regain the consciousness of the great chain of life from which he cannot be separated. He must understand that all creation has its value…. Life should only be negated when it is for a higher value and purpose—not merely in selfish or thoughtless actions. What then results for man is not only a deepening of relationships, but a widening of relationships.[5]

Doctor Schweitzer returned to Lambaréné in 1924 and spent the rest of his life working in the mission hospital. His wife and his daughter, Rhena, stayed behind in Europe due to Helene's failing health but the couple corresponded regularly. With funds earned from royalties, concerts, lectures and donations from friends and benefactors, Doctor Schweitzer continued building the hospital in Lambaréné. By the 1960s, the complex had expanded to seventy units, providing care to five hundred hospitalized patients.

At Lambaréné, Schweitzer was physician and surgeon, pastor, administrator, writer, musician, tour guide and welcoming host to a steady stream of visitors. As his fame spread worldwide, numerous honors, including the Goethe Prize of Frankfurt, and honorary doctorates from various universities, were conferred on him. When he was awarded the Nobel Peace Prize on December 10, 1953, he built a leprosarium with the $33,000 in prize money.

Like his friend Albert Einstein, Doctor Schweitzer was profoundly disturbed by the advent of nuclear weapons and the bombings of Hiroshima and Nagasaki. In 1957, he issued "A Declaration of Conscience," and in 1958, wrote the book *Peace or Atomic War?* In his eighties, he tirelessly wrote and lectured on the dangers of nuclear proliferation and the threat of nuclear war.

Retired from surgery, Albert Schweitzer continued to supervise his hospital until his death at the age of ninety on September 4, 1965. Albert and Helene are buried on the hospital grounds of their beloved Lambaréné.

Speaking of his friend, Albert Einstein remarked that Doctor Albert Schweitzer, "did not preach and did not warn and did not dream that his example would be an ideal and comfort to innumerable people. He simply acted out of inner necessity."[6]

Saint Elizabeth of Hungary
(1 2 0 7 – 1 2 3 1)

Elizabeth, the daughter of King Andrew II and Queen Gertrude was born in Pressburg, Hungary, in 1207. Saint Hedwig was her maternal aunt. Saint Elizabeth (Isabel) of Portugal was her great-niece.

As was common practice at that time, Elizabeth, at age four, was promised in marriage to the future prince of Thuringia by political agreement. The young Elizabeth was brought to the court of Thuringia in southern Germany to live in the castle of Wartburg. Despite her royal upbringing, Elizabeth was inclined to prayer and self-mortification early in life. In 1216, when the oldest son and heir to the throne died, Elizabeth was betrothed to the second son, Ludwig.

In 1221, Ludwig and Elizabeth were married. Despite its politically mandated beginning, their marriage turned genuinely happy as the couple truly loved each other. Ludwig approved of his wife's religious practices, which displeased members of the royal family.

With Elizabeth's sponsorship the Franciscans established a monastery in Eisenach in 1225; Brother Rodeger became her spiritual director and instructed Elizabeth on the ideals of Saint Francis of Assisi. While she could practice humility, patience, charity and other virtues, voluntary poverty as taught by Saint Francis was difficult to attain because of her royal standing. Alternatively, Elizabeth dressed simply and sought other ways of practicing poverty.

In the spring of 1226, when floods and famine devastated Thuringia, Ludwig was away in Italy attending the Diet at Cremona. Elizabeth took control of the situation and organized relief efforts to all territories under her husband's jurisdiction. In order to directly care for those affected, she opened near the Wartburg castle a hospital with twenty-eight beds, visiting patients daily to attend to their needs. She also attended daily to about a thousand people affected by the disaster.

The year following the catastrophe, Ludwig embarked on a crusade to the Holy Land but fell ill and died. The news did not reach Elizabeth until after the birth of their third child. Upon receiving the tragic news, Elizabeth cried out: "The world is dead to me, and all that was joyous in the world."[7]

Elizabeth left Wartburg under circumstances that are historically unclear. Her children were reportedly taken elsewhere. In 1228, on Good Friday, Elizabeth formally renounced the world in a ceremony at the Franciscan house in Eisenach and received the habit of the Third Order of Saint Francis, joining the ranks of the first Franciscan tertiaries of Germany.

In the summer of 1228 she built the Franciscan hospital at Marburg and upon its completion dedicated all her time and effort to the care of patients, especially those afflicted with the most severe illnesses. Elizabeth passed away at the age of twenty-four, at Marburg, on November 17, 1231 and her remains were buried in the hospital church.

Soon after her death, miraculous healings occurred through her intercession. On May 28, 1235, the "greatest woman of the German Middle Ages" was canonized by Pope Gregory IX. In August 1235, construction of the church of St. Elizabeth at Marburg began. In 1249 her remains were transferred to the choir of the church where pilgrimages became very popular.

During the Reformation, in 1539, a local ruler ended the pilgrimages and removed the relics of Saint Elizabeth, but the local people continued to venerate her. Saint Elizabeth is usually portrayed as a princess distributing alms to the poor or carrying roses. According to legend, as she went secretly on a mission of mercy, the bread she was hiding turned into roses.

QUESTIONS FOR REFLECTION

1. Do you feel an "inner necessity" as Albert Schweitzer did? What is it? What does it compel you to do?

2. If you do not feel an "inner necessity," what do you think compels you or urges you to care for others? Do you ever stop to think about why it is you do what you do?

SPIRITUAL EXERCISE

Make a list of things you can do for your hospital, for your community, perhaps for your region. Start with little things—minor projects. Get going with projects on your own, or with the help of friends. Renew your list at least annually.

PRAYER

It is you who light my lamp;
> the LORD, my God, lights up my darkness.
By you I can crush a troop,
> and by my God I can leap over a wall.
—Psalm 18: 28–29

notes

[1] Association Internationale de l'Oeuvre du Docteur Albert Schweitzer de Lambarene (AISL), July 9, 2001, p. 1.

[2] AISL, p. 1.

[3] AISL, p.1.

[4] AISL, p. 2.

[5] AISL, p. 5.

[6] AISL, p. 6.

[7] Ellsberg, p. 501.

eight

LAZARUS ON CHRISTMAS

Hope and Perseverance

"If you are able!—All things can be done for the one who believes."

—MARK 9:23

He was clearly dying, if he hadn't already. His face was pale, expressionless and greasy from the sweat. His arms were immobile, his legs swollen, his body rigid. The EKG monitor above the head of the bed showed a slow rhythmic pattern. He had a faint pulse. Oxygen was delivered by a ventilator.

His distraught wife quietly sobbed by the bedside. Laying her head on her left arm, she reached out and rubbed his arm and chest, careful not to dislodge the electrodes and intravenous lines.

Yesterday, she had brought their seven-year-old boy to visit his papa, perhaps for the last time. They both lit a votive candle later in the Orthodox church, and said more prayers. In the ICU, she had created a small altar where she and her family left a rosary, religious cards, prayer books, flowers and family photos.

What else could she do, except to wait in hope, to pray even more?

Sergei was a good father, a loving husband. He was happy when their immigration papers were finally approved and they could leave their

Soviet-controlled homeland. It would have been nice if he had found work as an engineer. But no company, at least in Southern California, was hiring immigrant engineers who spoke fluent Russian, but very little English. The job of repairing air conditioning units was not exactly his idea of engineering. But he could do it well and it paid good money. With it, he could rent a nice apartment, buy a reliable used car and afford to take his family to Seaworld and Disneyland. Life in the United States was good.

Sergei was working on an exterior air condition unit high on the seventh floor when he lost his footing and slipped off the ledge. He fell, head first, landing on bushes before striking the pavement.

His brain was mush. The paramedics quickly responded to the call, the trauma team of nurses and doctors resuscitated him rapidly and transported him to the operating room where neuro- and trauma surgeons attended to his injuries. We were able to evacuate most, if not all, of the blood clots and stop the brain hemorrhage. But, as expected, his brain swelled up and extruded beyond the craniotomy.

He was kept in a pharmacologically induced barbiturate coma for days, to let his damaged brain rest and recover. He was hyperventilated to keep his carbon dioxide level low so that brain edema would subside. He was supported with total parenteral nutrition and covered with broad-spectrum antibiotics. Physical therapy to keep his joints and extremities from contracture was started. The ICU team of nurses, critical care physicians, nutritionists, cardiologists, pulmonologists, trauma surgeons, neurologists, neurosurgeons and infectious disease specialists were constantly on the lookout for complications—blood loss, coagulopathy, pneumonia, pulmonary embolism, wound infection, urinary tract infection. All vital organs—his heart, lungs, liver, kidneys—were monitored and supported.

What else could be done? Sergei had "survived" the horrendous injuries incurred in the fall but he was transitioning into what neurologists call a "persistent vegetative state."

Weeks later, when clinical progress had reached a plateau, a Russian translator was summoned and a family conference arranged. Sergei's wife was ushered into the conference room. You could see that she dreaded the words she was about to hear. She could not understand English but she sensed what the physicians were communicating before the translator made them comprehensible in her native tongue.

From all indications, her husband had suffered an irreversible injury to his brain. Very likely, he would end up in a nursing home, breathing on his own and perhaps opening his eyes but unable to recognize his family, totally dependent on skilled nurses and staff to keep him clean and comfortable, fed through a nasogastric tube or through a tube in his stomach.

It was too much to bear; she broke down in tears. When she had recovered, she genuinely thanked the nurses, the physicians, the social workers and the entire team who had worked to save her husband's life.

There is nothing as dreadful in medicine as breaking that kind of news to a family, a spouse, a parent, brothers, sisters. We did everything we could, but it was just not good enough. A gut-wrenching feeling, as if your insides are sliced through and through with a pervading sense of failure, disappointment and inadequacy, creeps up on you. What can you say to the family that would make it any easier for them?

Sergei's wife did not want him taken off the respirator—neither did we, though one neurologist was convinced that keeping him alive was an exercise in futility.

Christmas was just around the corner. It was decided that we stay the course, and continue to aggressively support Sergei. The trauma team continued to treat him as if he would wake up in a few days instead of languish in persistent coma. We had already taken him out of the barbiturate-induced coma. The ventilator was attached to a healing tracheostomy (surgical opening in the windpipe). Food was delivered through a gastric tube. The pulmonologist "bronched" him regularly, that is, passed a flexible scope through the trachea and cleaned the "pulmonary tree" of potentially harmful mucus and prevented the collapse of fragile lung cells. His central lines, IVs, and Foley catheter, were routinely changed to prevent infection. Then, one morning, toward Christmas, the "miracle" happened. Sergei opened his eyes and seemed to recognize his wife! He could not speak, not with the tracheostomy tube in his windpipe. But his look was enough to release a rushing torrent of joyfulness to her grieving heart!

Sergei started moving his hands, his toes, he started "overriding" the ventilator—he sucked in a breath even before the ventilator recycled to pump oxygen into his lungs. Soon, we were able to take him off the machine. His voice was hoarse and raspy but he spoke his first words in Russian and greeted us with a weak smile.

With assistance, he sat up in bed; his eyes became more focused and alive. His Russian words extended into phrases, then sentences. Physical therapists eventually got him out of bed and into a wheelchair. He got out of the ICU and into the regular surgical ward. As his Russian became more fluent, he started speaking in English!

Sergei eventually walked out of the hospital, his wife and son beaming by his side. When I saw him in the clinic, a week later, he said he was all right—except for an occasional headache.

 VIRTUOUS HEALERS WHO EXEMPLIFIED
HOPE AND PERSERVERENCE

Saint Luke the Evangelist
(AD 10–84)

Saint Luke is honored as patron saint of physicians and surgeons and recognized as the author of one of the four Gospels and the Acts of the Apostles. History otherwise yields scant information about the faithful missionary and tireless evangelist whom Saint Paul refers to in Colossians 4:14 as "Luke, the beloved physician."

The name Lucas is likely an abbreviation of Lucanus which is found in some Old Latin manuscripts of the Gospel. According to the historian Eusebius, Luke was born of Greek parents in Antioch, the capital of Syria. He was not Jewish and his account of the life and ministry of Jesus Christ was primarily directed to the Gentiles.

There is no historical account as to his education but Saint Luke is regarded as a physician by Eusebius, Saint Jerome, Saint Irenaeus and the second-century writer Caius. We sense Saint Luke's educational background in his literary style and rich vocabulary. It is speculated that he may have studied medicine at the famous school in Tarsus, rather than in Alexandria or Athens, and may have met Saint Paul there. From his knowledge of the eastern Mediterranean, it is conjectured that he may have worked for some time as a ship doctor. In any case, Saint Luke's writings indicate that he was well educated and widely traveled.

Saint Luke and Saint Paul met at Troas around AD 51. Saint Luke then accompanied Paul during part of his second (AD 50–53) and third (AD 54–58) missionary journeys. After Saint Paul was released from prison, Luke left Philippi and reunited with Paul in Troas in AD 58. They traveled together to Miletus, Tyre, Caesarea, then to Jerusalem.

Saint Luke and Aristarchus accompanied Saint Paul during the stormy crossing of the Mediterranean Sea from Crete to Malta on their way to Rome. Luke stayed with Paul when he was tried and imprisoned in Rome in the year 61. When his followers deserted him during his final imprisonment, Saint Paul wrote to Timothy: "I have fought the good fight, I have finished the race, I have kept the faith...do your best to come to me soon, for Demas...has deserted me.... Only Luke is with me" (2 Timothy 4:7, 9, 11).

Saint Luke's reputation as a painter cannot be authenticated but a picture of the Blessed Virgin Mary in Santa Maria Maggiore Basilica in

Rome is traditionally attributed to him. It makes sense to assume that, through the centuries, Christian artists were inspired by Saint Luke's graphic descriptions of such scriptural scenes as the Annunciation, the Visitation, the Nativity, the shepherds in the fields and the Presentation.

The accounts of Saint Luke's life after Paul's martyrdom are sketchy, at best. He may have preached in Macedonia, Dalmatia and Italy. According to tradition, he died at the age of seventy-four around AD 84 in Achaia or Greece where he had retired to write the Acts of the Apostles and what many scholars consider the most literary of the four Gospels.

The Gospel According to Saint Luke reveals Jesus' humanity, particularly his concern for the poor and the marginalized. In his account of the Sermon on the Mount, for instance, the beatitudes begin with "Blessed are the poor" instead of "Blessed are the poor in spirit."

The traditional Hail Mary is taken from Saint Luke's account of the Annunciation: "Greetings, favored one! The Lord is with you" (Luke 1:28), and the Visitation: "Blessed are you among women, and blessed is the fruit of your womb" (Luke 1:42).

The parable of the Prodigal Son (Luke 15:11–32), which illustrates God's mercy and forgiveness, is found only in Luke's Gospel.

Saint Luke is often represented with an ox or a calf, symbols of sacrifice, and he is the patron saint of surgeons.

Doctor Tom Dooley
(1927–1961)

"I am only one, but I am one. I cannot do everything, but I can do something. What I can do, I ought to do, and what I ought to do, by the grace of God, I will do."[1]

—TOM DOOLEY

Thomas Anthony Dooley was born in St. Louis, Missouri on January 17, 1927. The eldest of three boys of devoutly Catholic parents, Thomas and Agnes Dooley, Tom attended parochial school. He was a gifted pianist and played for the St. Louis orchestra well enough that his family encouraged him to pursue a career in music. But Tom was thinking of becoming a doctor and, after graduating from St. Louis University High School where he excelled in swimming and track, he enrolled at the University of Notre Dame.

He enjoyed his college years in South Bend, Indiana, but did not care much for the strict discipline imposed by the Holy Cross Fathers. In a letter to Notre Dame President Father Theodore Hesburgh on December 2, 1960 a few weeks before he died, he wrote:

> Notre Dame is twice on my mind…and always in my heart. That Grotto [of the Blessed Virgin Mary at Lourdes] is the rock to which my life is anchored. Do the students ever appreciate what they have, while they have it? I know I never did. Spent most of my time being angry at the clergy at school…10 P.M. bed check, absurd for a 19 year old veteran….[2]

Cutting short his undergraduate studies at Notre Dame, Tom Dooley enlisted in the United States Navy Medical Corps in 1944. After an honorable discharge from the Navy, he enrolled at St. Louis University, graduating with an M.D. degree in 1953. He returned to the Navy for medical internship and postgraduate training. Commissioned as lieutenant, Doctor Dooley participated in "Passage to Freedom," an operation which evacuated over half a million Vietnamese refugees in August, 1954. Later, he served as medical officer for a Preventive Medicine Unit and supervised the refugee camps in Haiphong.

Doctor Tom Dooley wrote about his experience in Vietnam in his first book, *Deliver Us From Evil* (1956), which became a best-seller. It was condensed in *Reader's Digest* and reprinted in eleven languages. The United States Chamber of Commerce named him among the ten

"Outstanding Men of America." He was awarded the Navy's Legion of Merit, becoming the youngest Medical Corps officer to receive such an honor, and was awarded the highest national decoration of the South Vietnamese government.

Doctor Dooley resigned from the Navy in 1956 to focus on building small hospitals in areas of southeast Asia where medical services were practically non-existent. Laos, with a population of three million, was one such area. Using royalties from his book, Doctor Dooley and three other Navy corpsmen opened St. Patrick's hospital in Nam Tha, a village near the Chinese border.

St. Patrick's hospital, built with local materials and patterned after the native architecture (bamboo walls and thatch roofs) had a fifteen-bed surgical ward, a medical floor stacked with palm leaf mats for thirty patients, a basic operating room and a cramped outpatient clinic. Doctor Dooley and his staff could not afford a generator so the fledgling hospital had no electricity, no X-ray machines, no plumbing, no air-conditioning. Yet, laboring under primitive conditions, Tom Dooley's persevering medical staff treated about a hundred patients daily, many with serious tropical and infectious diseases such as dysentery, diphtheria, smallpox and tuberculosis. Patients were often severely malnourished and highly susceptible to various other illnesses.

Doctor Dooley worked in Laos from 1957 to 1961. He built hospitals in Vang Vieng, Luang, Nam Tha and Muang Sing. Criticized for practicing "nineteenth-century medicine," Doctor Dooley pointed out that, without access to medical services, people in the underserved regions often resorted to very primitive remedies, such as native witchcraft and magic.

In lectures throughout the United States, Doctor Dooley urged young men and women to dedicate their lives to others. He reminded his medical colleagues to visualize Jesus Christ in every patient, regardless of race, gender, economic or social status.

Questioned by colleagues in the U.S. as to why he was involved in rudimentary medicine halfway around the world, Doctor Tom Dooley replied,

All of us have the same quiet, inner joy that you have when you see your patient's eyes light up just a little bit because of you. But take that patient and put him in a hospital, in a high mountain valley, half a world away, where without you he has black magic or sorcery: you heal him and the glow inside of you is...a thing full of wonder.[3]

To advance his plans to establish clinics and hospitals in southeast Asia, Doctor Dooley founded the Medical International Cooperation Organization, or MEDICO. In a series of lectures, he raised one million dollars to jumpstart MEDICO. Doctor Dooley wrote his second book, *The Edge of Tomorrow* (1958), which chronicled the construction of hospitals in Nam Tha, Vang Vieng and Luang. In his third and last book, *The Night They Burned the Mountain* (1960), he wrote about the establishment of the hospital in Muang Sing and about his trip down the Nam Tha River to deliver medicines to inhabitants along the river.

In August 1959, Doctor Dooley was diagnosed with malignant melanoma and underwent surgery.

On June 5, 1960, he received an honorary Doctor of Science degree from his alma mater, the University of Notre Dame. In attendance at the ceremony was the Archbishop of Milan, Cardinal Giovanni Baptiste Montini who would later become Pope Paul VI.

In December 1960, Doctor Tom Dooley wrote to Notre Dame President Father Ted Hesburgh from Hong Kong,

More do I think of one divine Doctor, and my own personal fund of grace. Is it enough?...

It has become pretty definite that the cancer has spread to the lumbar vertebrae, accounting for all of the back problems over the last two months.

I have monstrous phantoms...as all men do. But I try to exorcise them with all the fury of the middle ages. And inside and outside the wind blows....
But when the time comes, like now, then the storm around me does not matter. The winds within do not matter. Nothing human or earthly can touch me. A wilder storm of peace gathers in my heart. What seems unpossessable I can possess. What seems unfathomable, I fathom. What is unutterable, I utter. Because I can pray. I can communicate. How do people endure anything on earth if they cannot have God?[4]

Thereafter, Doctor Tom Dooley was life-flighted to Sloan-Kettering Memorial Hospital in New York. By then, the melanoma had metastasized to his lungs, liver and brain. After receiving Extreme Unction (the sacrament of the sick and dying), he died peacefully on January 18, 1961, a day after his thirty-fourth birthday. This exemplary physician gave everything he had to medicine and mankind.

QUESTIONS FOR REFLECTION

1. What do you consider your greatest accomplishments in life? Do you think others can say of you what they said of Tom Dooley, that no one was equaled in the "exhibition of courage, self-sacrifice, faith in his God and his readiness to serve his fellow man"?

2. Consider some of your most proud accomplishments in the past. What if any legacy do you think you will leave to your progeny?

SPIRITUAL EXERCISE

This exercise was inspired and written for an unpublished manuscript *Tending the Soul* by Father Luke Dougherty, O.S.B., from the Prince of Peace Abbey in Oceanside, California. It is designed to help you look over your own life and review not only your accomplishments, but your failures as well, including the people who impacted your life most. This exercise will help you answer the questions for reflection.

Take an 8 ½" x 11" piece of paper and turn it sideways. Next, take a ruler and draw a line from side to side. Go to the beginning of the line (on the left) and write the year of your birth, then go to the other end of the line and put the year that you estimate to be the year of your death.

Figure 1. Time Line

For example, I was born in 1929. Looking back at my history, family history, my health, the patterns of my life of which I am aware, I can expect to live to the age of eighty. So, at the other end I would write 2010.

The next thing is to position the present year, for example, 2009, along the time line (see Figure 1). By so doing, you have given some thought to your lifeline—when it started and when your journey upon this earth might come to an end. Most importantly, you bring to the forefront your relationship with that all-important day, the last day of your journey upon this earth.

Write on the paper a list of all the significant people in your life up to the present time. By "significant people" I mean those who in some way or another, positively or negatively, changed your life. You may begin with your parents, your siblings, grandparents, aunts, uncles, teachers. After each person's name, put a plus (+), or a minus (-), indicating whether they were a positive or a negative influence.

Next, make another list much like the people list above; but this time, make a list of events in your life that affected you very deeply—events which changed the course of your life or transformed your life in some noteworthy way or another. Again, indicate whether the event was a positive or a negative experience.

Having made the list of people and events, go back and put those events chronologically along the time line, beginning with your birth and working through your childhood, teenage, young adult, adult, on to your mature years (if you are already there) and to a second career phase (if you've reached that point in your life).

Putting all of these along this time line will give you the ability to see all your significant moments at a glance. Then, proceed with a graph (see example in Figure 2). If it was a good year, a good time, trace above the line; if it was a bad time, a difficult time, go below the line. You will find that over a lifetime you will see a pattern emerge.

Figure 2 – Time Line

2009

1929   2010

Set aside some time to sit down to write, slowly and prayerfully, the story of your life as you can remember it. It can be written in a simple or in a detailed format. In any case, this is a story that you will certainly identify with because it is your own. But most importantly, as the story unfolds, you will discover very definite messages concerning your life, the nature and pattern of your journey, and about God.

PRAYER

My Lord God,

I have no idea where I am going.

I do not see the road ahead of me.

I cannot know for certain where it will end.

Nor do I really know myself,

and the fact that I think that I am doing Your will,

does not mean that I am actually doing so.

But I believe that the desire to please You

does in fact please You.
And I hope I have that desire
in all I am doing.
I hope that I will never do anything
apart from that desire.
And I know that if I do this,
You will lead me by the right road,
even though I may know nothing about it.

Therefore, I will trust You always,
though I may seem to be lost
and in the shadow of death.
I will not fear,
for You are ever with me,
and will never leave me—
to face my perils alone…[5]

notes

[1] From "Dr. Tom Dooley" in *NDVision*, available at www.nd.edu.

[2] Tom Dooley's letter to Father Hesburgh, University of Notre Dame archives.

[3] "Top 100 Catholics of the Century," *Daily Catholic*, August 10, 1999, Vol. 10, no. 149, p. 6 available at http://www.dailycatholic.org.

[4] Doctor Tom Dooley's Letter to Father Hesburgh, University of Notre Dame Archives.

[5] Thomas Merton, *Thoughts in Solitude* (New York: Farrar, Straus and Giroux), p. 79.

nine

COFFEE BREAK
Faith and Spirituality

"Do not let your hearts be troubled. Believe in God, believe also in me."

—JOHN 14:1

Does a good and effective physician necessarily have to be spiritual—to be a man or woman of faith?

Does the task of ministering to the sick and suffering, and of saving lives, contribute to one's personal growth? As a consequence of spending our days (and nights) caring for those who suffer, will we, in the process, become better individuals—more tolerant, more understanding, more sympathetic, more prudent, more spiritual?

What is the link between medicine, idealism, humanism and spirituality? What is the common thread that binds them? What, in the deepest core of our being, invites us, attracts us, compels us to care for our suffering brothers and sisters, to strive for the noblest, purest, most selfless goals, to interconnect with our fellow human beings, to reach out for the transcendent, to explore the mystery that gives meaning to our lives in the midst of so much suffering, pain, agony and death?

Did I become a physician or a nurse because I deliberately wanted to be one? Was it an accident, a convergence of circumstances, fate? Or was

I specifically chosen by Divine Providence (from eternity) to carry on the work of healing the sick, of alleviating pain, of saving lives?

Where is God in my work? How is God acting in my daily tasks? Can God work through me? Do I allow him to? Or do I prefer to work on my own and not bother about the spiritual or Divine aspect of my work?

Is God acting through me when I prescribe an antibiotic to cure an infection, when I open an abdomen to relieve an intestinal obstruction, when I fix a broken bone, when I deliver a newborn baby?

Do I see my patients through human eyes alone or do I also recognize the suffering Christ in my patients?

On the final year of my general surgical residency, I recall having coffee with one of my interns, after a typically exhausting Sunday night. The ER was winding down, and the ICU patients remained fairly stable. We lingered at the hospital cafeteria, grateful for the rare break. We did not want to think about Monday morning—we already knew it was going to have a fully loaded surgical schedule.

"You have a deep faith in God, don't you?" It was a rhetorical question.

My intern took another sip and sighed, "You are lucky, you know."

Silently, I cradled the cup of coffee in my hands.

"In tough situations, like the case we had this morning, I would have despaired." A cervical spine fracture had come in to the ER. The young man had been shot at close range in the neck. He was completely paralyzed from the neck down. We stabilized him on a respirator after emergency surgery.

"I can see myself in that patient," my intern continued. "Man, what is there left to do? That's it. His life is shattered!"

"You think so?" I asked.

"You're just lucky you can see beyond the tragedy. You believe in something? Some higher power, a God. Someone out there who can set things right...do great things. Things we can't even imagine. That's it, right?

When times are tough, you can go into a church, light a candle, and pray to your God.... Does God really solve your problems? Or do you just kind of psychologically get settled, adjust to the situation, you know?"

"That's why it's called the gift of faith," I said. "It's worthwhile to have."

"That's what I mean," my intern's eyes looked sad. "I am an atheist, you know. My parents were both atheists. I was brought up without any sense of religion. No matter how badly I wanted to, I could not believe in, much less adore or worship a God.... It's OK most days. But when the going gets tough, I have nowhere to turn."

"Can you give it a good college try—believing in God?" I asked. "Einstein said that if you think hard enough and look around you, you will have to believe in a Supreme Being.... If I remember correctly, he said something like: There are two ways to live your life: One as though nothing is a miracle, the other as though everything is."

"Yeah, well...maybe."

We finished our coffee in silence.

  VIRTUOUS HEALERS WHO EXEMPLIFIED
FAITH AND SPIRITUALITY

Saint John of the Cross
(1542–1591)

"The reason the soul suffers so intensely for God at this time is that she is drawing nearer to him; so she has greater experience within herself of the void of God, of very heavy darkness, and of spiritual fire that dries up and purges her so that thus purified she may be united with him...until God introduces her into his divine splendors through transformation of love...."[1]

—SAINT JOHN OF THE CROSS

The great Spanish mystic and theologian Juan de Yepes was born in Fontiveros, a small town located between Madrid and Salamanca, in 1542. His father, Gonzalo, was a silk merchant who was disowned by his family when he married a poor weaver, Catalina Alvarez. Juan was the youngest of their three boys.

Papa Gonzalo passed away when Juan was only two years old. Second son Luis died thereafter. After the eldest boy Francisco got married, Catalina relocated to Medina del Campo, where she enrolled Juan in an elementary school for poor children.

Juan apprenticed in a variety of trades and served as acolyte at a nearby Augustinian monastery, La Magdalena. Later in his teens, Juan was recruited to work as a hospital attendant by Don Alonso Alvarez, administrator of the hospital in Medina. Juan's characteristic gentleness and patience impressed the hospital staff and endeared him to his patients.

Juan entered the town's Jesuit college at age seventeen and then attended the University of Salamanca to study art, philosophy and theology. Recognized as a brilliant and diligent student, he was appointed prefect of studies. Academic life, however, particularly as it pertained to the pursuit of honors and the collection of titles, did not appeal to him. He decided to become a Carmelite novice and was ordained a priest in 1576 at the age of twenty-five. During a visit to Medina to celebrate Mass, the newly ordained Carmelite priest was introduced to the mother superior, Madre Teresa de Jesus—the future Saint Teresa of Avila, who was fifty-two at the time and on the verge of radically reforming the Carmelite Order. Saint Teresa persuaded Fray Juan, who was thinking of joining the Carthusian Order, to join her cause instead.

After completing a year of theology in Salamanca in 1568, John of the Cross became actively involved in the Carmelite reform movement with Saint Teresa. With two other priests, he started the first Discalced Carmelite house in Duruelo. In 1571 he became rector of the university college of Alcala de Henares. Saint Teresa was instrumental in having him appointed confessor of the Convent of the Incarnation in Avila.

A tragic point in his life occurred on December 2, 1577, when John of the Cross was kidnapped from Avila and imprisoned in Medina del Campo. Accused of rebellion by traditional Carmelites who protested the reform movement, John of the Cross was held prisoner there until his release was ordered by the papal nuncio. Two years later, he was again abducted by opposition factions. Handcuffed and blindfolded, he was sequestered in a monastery in Toledo.

Father John was of short stature, about four-eleven, yet there was hardly room for him to move around in his six- by ten-foot cell. In prison, his meals consisted mainly of bread, sardines and water. He was abused and subjected to frequent beatings. It was during nine months of solitary confinement in a dark prison cell that he wrote the first part of his "Spiritual Canticle." This period of intense suffering served as impetus for his most famous work, *The Dark Night of the Soul*. Its classic opening reads:

One dark night,
fired with love's urgent longings
—ah, the sheer grace! —
I went out unseen,
my house being now all stilled.[2]

One night, malnourished and emaciated, John unscrewed the door lock of his cell and lowered himself from the city wall using a rope made out of bedcover remnants. With only the tattered clothes on his back and clutching a worn notebook of his poems, he sought refuge in a reform monastery in Toledo. Nuns who were sympathetic to the reform movement transferred him to a hospital in Santa Cruz where he was well protected and allowed to recuperate.

After his recovery, he was appointed vicar of the reform convent of El Calvario, a monastery in Andalusia. In less than a year he established the university college in Baeza and became its rector. As his situation normalized, John dedicated himself even more to his favorite ministry: spiritual direction. Remarkably, he forgave his kidnappers and never complained about his maltreatment in prison. Pain and suffering, he pointed out, were not misfortunes but values to be treasured when experienced with and for Christ.

Furthermore, John of the Cross considered physical suffering akin to spiritual suffering. The "dark night of the soul"—that stage in the spiritual life when God seems hidden and the soul feels abandoned—if endured with faith, hope and love, may lead the soul to a profound transformation and, ultimately, to ecstatic union with God.

In 1582, Father John of the Cross was elected prior of Los Martires in Granada. There, his ministry of spiritual direction flourished and he began composing most of his classical works, including the commentaries on *Ascent of Mount Carmel* and *The Dark Night of the Soul*.

In 1585, he was elected vicar provincial of Andalusia and established several new monasteries. Three years later, he was elected first councilor to the vicar general of his order. As head of the monastery, he was known to provide his sick friars with the best medical care possible. It is told that at one time, when a doctor complained that the only medicine available to effectively treat a sick friar was too expensive, Father John, despite financial hardship, bought the expensive medicine and administered the remedy himself.

On frequent visits to monasteries under his jurisdiction, he first prayed before the Blessed Sacrament and immediately visited the sick. He cheerfully made rounds and happily visited patients who enjoyed his company. Father John often taught that "the more you love God the more you desire that all people love and honor him and as the desire grows you work harder toward that end, both in prayer and in all other possible works."[3]

He taught that the spiritual life, extending from the rudimentary practices of Christian living to the highest peaks of mysticism, encompasses both active and passive elements. Thus, while steadfastly pursuing a contemplative life, he actively participated in many tasks in the community, such as choir singing, kitchen chores, gardening, altar decorating, construction work, brick-laying, floor scrubbing, visiting the sick and hearing confessions.

In 1591, tragedy struck again when John was deprived of his authority and stripped of his administrative positions. He was to be banished to Mexico but he fell ill before the trip. Ostracized by his fellow Carmelites, he sought refuge in the solitude of La Penuela in Andalusia. There, he contracted an infection, developed gangrene of his lower extremities and had to be transferred to the reform convent of Ubeda for medical care. On December 14, 1591, alone and abandoned by his own congregation, John of the Cross died a lonely death after receiving the last rites on his way "to sing Matins in heaven."

On January 22, 1675, Pope Clement X beatified John of the Cross. Pope Benedict XIII canonized him on December 27, 1726. Pope Pius XI, on August 24, 1926, declared him doctor of the church for his invaluable contribution to mystical theology. Saint John of the Cross is also recognized as one of Spain's greatest poets.

Doctor Adrienne von Speyr
(1902–1967)

Adrienne von Speyr was born on September 20, 1902, in the city of La Chaux-de-Fonds, Switzerland. She was the second of four siblings born to Theodor von Speyr, an ophthalmologist and Laure Girard. Her younger brother Wilhelm (1905–1978) was also a physician.

Adrienne had a difficult relationship with her mother but was close to her pious and doting grandmother. She was also devoted to her father who often took her along to the hospital to make rounds. Adrienne was a diligent and bright student and was often asked to substitute for her teachers.

Her mystical experiences happened early. At the age of six, Adrienne reportedly had an encounter with Saint Ignatius of Loyola while walking up a street on Christmas Eve. In November 1917, at the age of fifteen, she experienced an apparition of the Blessed Virgin Mary surrounded by angels and saints. Shortly after her conversion in 1940, at the age of thirty-eight, a dazzling light appeared in front of her car, as she was driving home, and she heard a voice say: *"Tu vivra au ciel et sur la terre"* (You shall live in heaven and on earth).[4]

Adrienne was often sick and suffered from frequent backaches. But, these disabilities did not keep her away from visiting and comforting hospitalized patients. Encouraged by her father, she attended secondary school intending to become a physician, a decision which her mother opposed.

Soon after her father died from a perforated gastric ulcer, Adrienne shifted to business school. But, she contracted tuberculosis and was sent to Leysin to be cared for by a relative, Doctor Charlotte Olivier. In Leysin, she spent her time reading and learning Russian. She also spent time praying in a Catholic chapel and there the beginnings of her gradual conversion from Protestantism took place.

Her mother wanted Adrienne to get a regular job and get married but she resolved to pursue her dream of becoming a physician. She paid for medical tuition by tutoring. In 1927, she met and fell in love with Emil Dürr, dean of the history department at the University of Basel, a widower with two young sons. Shortly after they married Adrienne passed her state medical board examinations, making history by becoming the first female physician in Switzerland.

Adrienne was known for her courage in rectifying injustices. It is reported that she once attended a medical workshop where the discussion centered on an intern who had erroneously ordered a lethal injection for a patient. The intern defended his position by blaming the nurse for administering the drug while the medical professor sided with the intern. In protest, Adrienne organized a boycott of the professor's classes until he was pressured to relocate elsewhere.

In 1934, Emil passed away and two years later Adrienne married Werner Kaegi, another professor of history at the University of Basel. In the succeeding years, Adrienne searched in vain for a Catholic priest who could assist her transition to Catholicism. In the fall of 1940, she met the Jesuit priest and Swiss theologian Father Hans Urs von Balthasar, who had recently been appointed chaplain at the University of Basel. On the Feast of All Saints, under Father von Balthasar's spiritual direction, Doctor Adrienne von Speyr was baptized and thereafter received the sacrament of confirmation.

It was a joyous time in her life. She had an enviable circle of friends and renowned Catholic intellectuals: Romano Guardini, Hugo Rahner, Erich Przywara, Henri de Lubac, Reinhold Schneider, Annette Kolb and Gabriel Marcel. Her medical practice was busy as she attended to sixty to eighty patients daily.

She happily treated poor patients for free even as her own physical ailments—diabetes, crippling arthritis and a heart attack—dragged her down. With Father von Balthasar's guidance, Adrienne founded a secular institute, the Community of Saint John.

Eventually, Adrienne received the stigmata. As Father von Balthasar wrote:

> [A] veritable cataract of mystical graces poured over Adrienne in a seemingly chaotic storm that whirled her in all directions at once. Graces in prayer above all: she was transported beyond all vocal prayer or self-directed meditation

upon in order to be set down somewhere after an indeterminate time with new understanding, new love and new resolutions...[including] an increasingly open and intimate association with Mary....[5]

She dictated her interpretation of several scriptural books to Father von Balthasar. Father von Balthasar recalled that she "seldom dictated for more than half an hour per day. During vacations she would occasionally dictate for two or three hours, but this was rare."[6] Their teamwork resulted in about sixty books in thirteen years, from 1940 to 1953.

By 1954 at the age of fifty-two Adrienne was so ill that she had to retire from medical practice. She spent her days in prayer, knitting clothing for the poor and reading. In 1964, at the age of sixty-two, she lost her eyesight due to uncontrolled diabetes. Her last months were filled with "continuous, merciless torture," wrote Father von Balthasar, "which she bore with great equanimity, always concerned about the others and constantly apologetic about causing me so much trouble."[7]

Doctor Adrienne von Speyr, physician, mystic, convert and spiritual writer, died on September 17, 1967, at the age of sixty-five, on the feast of another mystic and physician, Saint Hildegard.

QUESTIONS FOR REFLECTION

1. Have you ever had a "dark night of the soul" as John of the Cross did? If so, when? Do you remember what precipitated it? How did you overcome it? Do you fear that it will ever happen again? Or do you welcome such trials of faith?

2. How well do you understand or know your faith? If you had to choose your faith today—if you, like Adrienne von Speyr, were not a Catholic—would you still choose this faith above all others? Why?

SPIRITUAL EXERCISE

Visit the Blessed Sacrament. Spend ten to fifteen minutes in quiet prayer. Make your visits a weekly habit.

Read a verse or two from the Old or New Testament. Read the passage slowly, prayerfully. Spend some time meditating on it. Try doing this exercise each day, if possible.

Act of Consecration to the Immaculate Heart of Mary

O Virgin Mary, my Mother, I give to your Immaculate Heart my body and my soul, my thoughts and my actions. I want to be just what you want me to be, and do just what you want me to do. I am not afraid because you are always with me. Help me to love your Son, Jesus, with all my heart and above all things. Take my hand in yours, so I can always be with you.

notes

[1] Kieran Kavanaugh, O.C.D., and Otilio Rodriguez, O.C.D., *The Collected Works of St. John of the Cross* (Washington, D.C.: ICS, 1991), p. 519.

[2] Kavanaugh and Rodriguez, *The Collected Works of St. John of the Cross*, p. 358.

[3] "A Portrait of the Saint" Austrian Province of the Teresian Carmel, http://www.ocd.or.at/ics/john/gen_7.html.

[4] "Doctor, Convert, and Mystic: The Life and Work of Adrienne von Speyr," http://www.ignatiusinisght.com/authors/adrienne_von_speyr.html.

[5] "Doctor, Convert, and Mystic."

[6] "Doctor, Convert, and Mystic."

[7] "Doctor, Convert, and Mystic."

ten

CHARLIE BROWN AND MANKIND

Humanism, Love and Charity

"This is my commandment, that you love one another as I have loved you."

—JOHN 15:12

Unlike my dear wife, I am not a big fan of the comic strip *Peanuts*. But there's one *Peanuts* cartoon I cannot forget. Charlie Brown matter-of-factly tells Lucie: "I love mankind. It's people I cannot stand."

Isn't that the truth? How resoundingly that remark echoes in the healthcare profession. We love to attend to those who come to us for help. We love to save people from devastating illness and death. We love to save the world.

But don't we complain when we have to drop everything we are doing to rush to the ER, the ICU or the OR? Why do we have to get out of a warm cozy bed in the middle of the night to examine someone's painful belly or attend to a gunshot wound or drain a messy abscess?

I certainly love surgery. It just stinks if I have to do it when the rest of the world (with the exception of paramedics, police, firemen and other third-shift workers) are tucked in bed with a nice book or watching a late-night show. How many play-off series and Monday Night Football games and championship golf and tennis matches have I missed because I had to be in the hospital?

Yet wasn't that the whole idea about going into medicine? Sickness does not take a holiday (it certainly has no regard for time zones or biorhythms), so those of us who have dedicated ourselves to combating disease and illness have no legitimate grounds for complaint.

For a long time I've been tempted to pull Charlie Brown aside to tell him: "I love mankind, Charlie Brown. I even love people. It's those darn interruptions I cannot stand!"

 ## VIRTUOUS HEALERS WHO EXEMPLIFIED HUMANISM, LOVE AND CHARITY

Saint Vincent de Paul

(1580–1660)

Vincent de Paul was born into a peasant family in the village of Pouy in Gascony, France, around 1580. He was educated by the Franciscan fathers at Acqs, studied humanities at Dax, and theology at the University of Toulouse. He was ordained to the priesthood in 1600, at age nineteen.

Following ordination, Father Vincent remained in or near Toulouse, working as a tutor and chaplain. Two incidents significantly affected the course of his life. In 1605, while traveling from Marseilles to Narbonne, he was taken captive by Turkish pirates and sold as a slave in Tunis. Two years into captivity, he escaped with his master, whom he had converted to Catholicism.

After a brief stay in Rome to resume his studies, he returned, in 1609, to Paris and eventually was assigned to the parish of Clichy. In 1612, he became chaplain to one of the wealthiest families in France, the renowned family of Philippe-Emmanuel de Gondy, Count of Goigny. As spiritual director to Madam de Gondy, he also tutored the couple's children and conducted missions in their large estate.

One day, Father Vincent was asked to hear the confession of a poor peasant. The dying penitent was deeply grateful, saying that he would have surely died in a state of mortal sin had it not been for his timely presence. The encounter touched Father Vincent profoundly and made him fully aware of the significance of his priestly vocation. Henceforth, he decided to focus on working to serve the poor, both physically and spiritually.

Pastoral, socioeconomic and political problems competed for Father Vincent's attention. He was concerned about the lack of formation of the clergy, about the physical and spiritual poverty in the rural areas, about inadequate care of the sick, about the neglect of orphans and the mentally ill, about the living conditions of prisoners and galley slaves, and about the fate of Christians held captive in North Africa. In pre-Revolutionary France, condemned convicts were typically leg-chained in damp dungeons and fed black bread and water. Malnourished, they often got sick, developed leg ulcers and were susceptible to many diseases. To rectify these conditions, he mustered his talents and efforts.

In 1625, Father Vincent de Paul established the Congregation of the Mission, a group of secular priests dedicated to the training of seminarians and secular priests and to conducting retreats and missions in towns and villages. They were called Lazarists because they occupied the Priory of Saint Lazarus. Later, they were called Padres Paules or Vincentians.

Prior to the French Revolution, the Congregation of the Mission directed fifty-three upper or grand seminaries (theological courses) and nine lesser seminaries (humanities courses) for the education of priests, comprising about a third of all seminaries in France. Father Vincent also personally conducted retreats for priests as well as for laymen. At the Priory of Saint Lazarus, approximately eight-hundred people came yearly for retreats and Father Vincent often gave up his own room to accommodate them.

He successfully persuaded wealthy women to get involved in the ministry to serve society's marginalized communities—the poor, the sick, widows, orphans—and organized them as the Ladies of Charity. With the help of a notable widow, Louise de Marillac, he founded the Daughters of Charity, dedicated primarily to children's education. For these remarkable women Father Vincent envisioned, "Their convent is the sickroom, their chapel the parish church, their cloister the streets of the city."[1]

Father Vincent de Paul established many hospitals, orphanages and mental institutions. He was directly involved in what is considered one of the greatest works of charity of the seventeenth century—the sheltering, feeding and work training of 40,000 people in Paris. Yet, his work was not confined to Paris. He was involved in so many charitable projects and religious missions throughout France that he became a legend in his time.

Nor were his charitable endeavors limited to the French; he directed his resources to Irish and English Catholics as well, displaced from their homelands. His soup kitchens reputedly fed 15,000 refugees daily. Yet, even as his fame spread, he remained a simple and humble priest. Often, he reminded his priests and nuns: "The poor are your masters and you are their servants."[2]

Vincent de Paul's charity extended way beyond the borders of France. He sent missionaries to Ireland, Scotland, the Hebrides, Poland and Madagascar from 1648 to 1660. Of all the missions overseas, none was closer to his heart than the work his missionaries performed for the slaves of Barbary because he had shared their fate. There were reportedly between 25,000 and 30,000 mostly Christian captives in Tunis, Algiers and Bizaerta. The missionaries brought comfort and relief to the slaves and served as messengers between them and their families. Through patient and tedious work, the missionaries successfully obtained the release of some 1,200 slaves.

Father Vincent de Paul died in Paris at the age of eighty on September, 27, 1660. He left a large volume of letters—at least 30,000—though only about 7,000 were preserved and 3,200 were eventually published.

In 1705, the superior-general of the Congregation of the Mission formally requested that the process of canonization begin. Vincent de Paul was beatified by Pope Benedict XIII on August 13, 1729, and canonized by Pope Clement XII on June 16, 1737.

Pope Leo XIII named Saint Vincent de Paul the patron saint of charitable societies. To honor and perpetuate the apostle of charity's work, the Saint Vincent de Paul Society, operating in many parishes today, was established in 1833 by Frederick Ozanam.

Saint Camillus de Lellis
(1550–1614)

Camillus was born in Bacchianico, Naples, in 1550. His mother was very religious and, like Saint Monica, prayed that someday her son would become a saint. His father, an officer in the Neapolitan and French military, did not share his wife's hopes for their son. After his mother passed away, Camillus followed in his father's footsteps; he joined the Venetian army to fight the Turks.

Camillus, the tall (six-foot-six) and athletic soldier of fortune, made his reputation with his quick temper and incessant gambling. Later, he fell in battle, sustaining a serious injury to his leg which developed a chronic infection. After his regiment disbanded, he went to San Giacomo in Rome. While undergoing prolonged treatment there, he worked as a servant and attendant in the hospital, occasionally performing nursing duties.

But his argumentative and disruptive behavior, in addition to what had become an addiction to gambling, got him fired from the hospital. With nowhere else to go, he reenlisted in the army. After the war was over, he needed a job after he had gambled away all his earnings. Fortunately, he got temporary employment as a laborer for the construction of a new building at the Capuchin monastery in Manfredonia. He became friends with the friars and soon he was admitted to the monastery as a lay brother. But the chronic wound in his leg became an issue and he was asked to leave.

His stint with the Capuchins, however, awakened a dormant spirituality; he vowed to stop gambling and lead a new life. Returning to San Giacomo, he devoted himself wholeheartedly to the care of the sick, seeing each patient in his care as if he or she were Christ incarnate. Camillus surprised everyone. He was a changed man and an exceptional nurse—caring, compassionate, prudent, practical and tireless. Advocating cleanliness, good nutrition and fresh air, he brought about "miraculous" cures and was soon promoted to superintendent of the hospital.

In his administrative position, he conceived of a religious order of lay infirmarians or an association of nurses whose care for patients would not be a manifestation solely of professional endeavor but, more profoundly, of a religious vocation. He consulted his spiritual director, Saint Philip Neri, who encouraged Camillus to pursue the project. However, the plan met with resistance and failed to materialize.

Recognizing his spiritual potential, Saint Philip Neri recommended that Camillus become a priest. He could bring the sacraments to his patients while providing them with nursing care. Camillus diligently took the required courses at the Jesuit College in Rome and, in 1584, at the age of thirty-four, Camillus de Lellis was ordained.

Father Camillus established the order of the Fathers of a Good Death and required its members to minister to plague-stricken patients admitted to hospitals or confined in their homes. Pope Sixtus V approved the religious congregation in 1586 and Father Camillus was elected its first superior general. Two years later, a congregation was established in

Naples. Two dedicated members of the community gave up their lives nursing terminal patients on a ship quarantined off the coast.

In 1591, Pope Gregory XIV formally recognized the Ministers of the Sick as a religious order and, in 1592, Pope Clement VIII allowed its members to be attired with a religious habit imprinted with a prominent red cross. The order attracted numerous members and volunteers who performed extraordinary medical and nursing services during outbreaks of the plague.

Reputed to have received the gift of miracles and of prophecy, Camillus was zealous in his ministry. Dedicated to nursing despite his chronic leg ailment, he did not wait for patients to arrive at the hospital doorsteps but roamed the city, seeking ill and dying patients. Besides constructing what would become a model hospital in Rome, Camillus established eight hospitals and fifteen religious houses all over Italy.

Father Camillus de Lellis, nurse and administrator extraordinaire, died in Genoa on July 14, 1614, at the age of sixty-four, while addressing his religious colleagues. He was buried in the altar of the church of St. Mary Magdalene in Rome. Declared blessed in 1742, he was canonized by Pope Benedict XIV in 1746.

In 1930, Pope Pius XI named Saint Camillus de Lellis, together with Saint John of God, principal co-patrons of nurses and of nurses' associations.

QUESTIONS FOR REFLECTION

1. Is your work motivated by selfless love and dedication? Or do you look for the recognition, the pat on the back, the prestige?
2. Can you truly say: "Lord, your will be done"? Rather than: "Yes, Lord, but please fit everything properly into my time and schedule"?

SPIRITUAL EXERCISE

Smile at everyone you see today. A kind word or compliment can't hurt, either.

PRAYER

My Prayer Before Making Rounds

Teach me, Lord, to love each person
without conditions, without reservations
regardless of time or circumstance.
Teach me, Lord, to give of myself fully
to the task of healing
the task you've given me.
Let me not find problems
where there are none.
Let me not look elsewhere
but only to the task at hand.
Your will, not mine, be done.

notes

[1] Ellsberg, p. 421.
[2] Ellsberg, p. 421.

eleven

THE KING'S TREE

Total Trust in Divine Providence

"Therefore I tell you, do not worry about your life, what you will eat or what you will drink, or about your body, what you will wear. Is not life more than food, and the body more than clothing?... Therefore do not worry...your heavenly Father knows that you need all these things.

"So do not worry about tomorrow, for tomorrow will bring worries of its own. Today's trouble is enough for today."

—MATTHEW 6:25, 31–32, 34

During a lecture delivered at the Congress of the American College of Surgeons, I listened to a distinguished professor who was chief of surgery of one of the most prestigious surgical training programs in the world. The speaker talked about what precisely transforms the competent surgeon into the "perfect surgeon." Comparing surgery to flying a plane, he divided any major operation into four segments: first, the meticulous pre-flight check list; second, the critical takeoff; third, the flight; and finally, the cautious landing.

A good surgeon, he remarked, was not unlike a good pilot. He has to know every phase, every detail of the surgical procedure. Anticipating every movement, he also has to control every aspect of the operation. Prior to the actual operation, the surgeon must possess detailed knowledge and comprehensive understanding of his patient's case. Then he envisions every step of the operation, from beginning to end. Prior to starting the operation, he checks that all necessary instruments are available, functioning properly, sterilized and ready to use. He makes sure the surgical team is up to speed. As the plane taxis in preparation for takeoff, so does surgery begin with induction of anesthesia, sterilization and draping of the surgical field. The plane takes off and, just like a good pilot, the surgeon focuses totally on the task at hand. He makes the incision of the abdomen or the chest, and observes closely as the anatomy opens up gently. He watches for bleeders, dissecting carefully, controlling every movement and anticipating every problem. The plane is airborne.

It goes without saying that the surgeon has thoroughly reviewed the operative techniques and maneuvers step by step, consulted an up-to-date atlas of surgical operations, run the operation in his mind over and over again. In today's laparoscopic environment, the surgeon must have watched the videotape or CD demonstration of the operation several times before stepping into the operating room.

Toward the end of the operation, the surgeon rechecks that the procedure is done as near to perfection as possible, checking for every possible oversight. After the incision is closed and a dressing applied, the patient is recovered from anesthesia and the surgery is complete. The plane lands. But the job is not quite done yet. The surgeon writes the postoperative orders and goes over these with the recovery room nurse. He checks back later to see if the patient is recovering well, with no signs of bleeding or respiratory compromise.

It is not time to go home and relax. He talks to the patient's family, updates them of the patient's progress, quelling their fears, assuring them that the patient is recovering well. He sticks around, checking on the patient's progress. He does not leave the hospital until he is absolutely sure that the operation has been a total success and the patient is completely stable.

That, in a nutshell, is the art and science of surgery. That is the way the complete surgeon practices his profession.

But does the surgeon really control everything? Does everything depend on his wits, intelligence, quickness, knowledge, determination or the deftness of his hands? Or is the Supreme Being, the Lord and Giver of Life, really in charge?

It is a humbling experience to realize that after four years of undergraduate studies, four years of medical school, endless nights of reading, multiple exams, five more years of surgical residency training, followed by more years of clinical practice, there is so much more that we simply do not know.

Reading Doctor Atul Gawande's *Complications: The Surgeon's Notes on an Imperfect Science* I am reminded that as many as 40 percent of autopsies reveal that the clinical diagnosis was in error. In other words, the pathologist finds out that the patient died of something other than what doctors thought the patient was suffering from. Missed diagnoses in 40 percent of patients was in some sense understandable in the age before sophisticated CT scans and MRIs. Yet, this figure has not changed for the last one hundred years.

No matter how careful, meticulous and compulsive we are, errors and complications do occur, adding streaks of silver in our hair and furrows to our forehead. They also teach us to be humble, and to acknowledge that we are not really in total control. Of course, this does not mean that the surgeon should let things slide by. We do need to study our cases comprehensively, check our instruments carefully, get the surgical team to work efficiently and perform our operations meticulously.

Ultimately, however, regardless of what we like to think, we are not in control, not totally anyway. God is the main surgeon. I am merely the assistant. The patient may have signed the consent for surgery to put his or her life into my hands. But I know there is the perfect surgeon, the Lord and Giver of Life.

How often am I confident that patients would get better if they only followed my instructions? How often do I forget that God is the primary healer? Can God actually heal through me? Or is that kind of healing historically confined to the Acts of the Apostles?

Sometime ago, a saintly nun, who taught me the rudiments of contemplative prayer, handed me a paper bearing the tale about a king and his favorite tree. She said it might help me understand God's ways a bit better.

The beautiful bamboo tree, with its long, wispy branches, swaying back and forth on windy days, was far and away the central attraction in the king's legendary garden. For years, the king would bring his family and friends for a picnic and spend the day in the garden. The king enjoyed watching his children frolic and play around the tree. He had planted and grown many other beautiful trees, but the bamboo tree was truly the king's favorite.

Yet one day, by royal decree, a band of wood cutters was dispatched to cut the bamboo tree down. The laborers unceremoniously sheared off the leaves, then cut off the tree's branches. The tree was stunned. How, in the world, could the king do such a thing? What had she done to make the king so mad?

The men chopped the tree down and sliced the trunks open in halves. They laid the bamboo strips on the ground and tied the long sticks together. Dragged down from its lofty perch, the tree was now flat on the ground—helpless, broken, useless.

As if this was not enough humiliation, the bamboo was drenched with buckets of water. Its arms and legs were not only smeared with mud, the tree was soaked wet and cold and left for dead. The tree was heart-broken. It had no idea why its fortunes had changed so drastically.

Days passed, weeks, then months. The king never showed up. The children stopped coming. The bamboo was alive, but barely. It would have been better off dead. No longer the king's favorite—down and out, dirty, cold and wet, abandoned, trodden on…the tree had lost everything it had been so proud of—beauty, respect, utility, self-esteem, influence. It had lost the three important Ps—possessions, power, prestige. It had degraded into a useless heap of chopped wood. What was left to live for?

One day, the king reappeared, along with hundreds of his subjects. He gave the order to start harvesting in the valley below. For, indeed, what was once barren land had now been transformed into a lush field, yielding abundant corn, wheat, crops and fruits, and all sorts of vegetables.

You could see the ecstatic faces of men, women and children. They danced with joy and praised their king. The wise king had the foresight to expect the drought's devastating effect. He had the courage to sacrifice his beloved bamboo tree so that a grand irrigation system could be constructed, the valley would flourish, and his subjects spared from starvation.

Only then did the bamboo tree understand what the wise and courageous king had done.

 VIRTUOUS HEALERS WHO EXEMPLIFIED TOTAL TRUST IN DIVINE PROVIDENCE

Saint Teresa of Avila

(1515–1582)

Born in Avila, Spain, on March 28, 1515, during the reign of King Ferdinand and Queen Isabella, Teresa was the third of the ten children of Don Alonso Sanchez de Cepeda and his second wife, Doña Beatriz Davila y Ahumada. A successful businessman, Don Alonso was also a deeply religious man. Teresa's grandfather, Juan Sanchez, a merchant from Toledo, was a "converso"—a Jew required by the Inquisition to convert to Catholicism, a fact which Teresa's future detractors would use against her. Doña Beatriz died at age thirty-three, leaving Don Alonso to raise fourteen-year-old Teresa and her nine brothers and sisters.

Teresa was a bright, charming and beautiful girl. She was also strong-willed and independent. The story is often told that when she was barely seven years old, she convinced her brother Rodrigo to travel with her to the territory of the Moors and offer their lives to God as martyrs. An uncle prevented premature martyrdom by returning the kids home before they got outside the city walls. Accurate or not, the anecdote reveals an adventurous, courageous and charismatic persona.

In 1531, Don Alonso enrolled Teresa at Santa Maria de Gracia to be educated by the Augustinian nuns. She was an outgoing student, involved in many extracurricular activities. Downtime was spent reading romantic stories and tales of chivalry. She was well on her way to becoming a popular debutante and prominent socialite in Avila when her friendship with one of the nuns, Doña Maria de Briseno, planted the seed of a religious vocation. A visit to her uncle, the hermit Don Pedro de Cepeda, led to her reading of the letters of Saint Jerome, which strengthened her determination to enter religious life.

Over the objections of her father, Teresa left home on November 2, 1535, and entered the Carmelite monastery of the Incarnation at the age of twenty. Later, Don Alonso relented, provided a dowry, and made the necessary financial arrangements to have Teresa lodged in a private room in the monastery.

Convents in Teresa's time were a hybrid of religious house and boarding school for wealthy young women. The Incarnation convent housed two hundred nuns, with their accompanying relatives and servants. Religious practices were observed, such as the recitation of the

Divine Office and chanting of the psalms, fasting, abstinence and periods of silence, but social life was barely restricted, if at all.

Two years after her profession, Teresa fell ill, probably from malaria. Physicians came up with no definite diagnosis and treatment so Teresa's father took her out of the convent and brought her to a faith-healer in Becedas who merely aggravated her condition. Teresa returned to Avila in the fall of 1538 where she was bedridden, paralyzed from the waist down. During this illness, her uncle Pedro de Cepeda introduced her to an influential book in her spiritual progress, the *Tercer Abecedario* of Francis of Osuna. It was through the intercession of Saint Joseph, Teresa later testified, that she was able to get out of bed and walk again after three years. Throughout the remainder of her life, however, she was subjected to a host of illnesses.

Teresa returned to Incarnation convent where she dedicated herself wholeheartedly to prayer. However, she found the practice difficult: "I tried as hard as I could to keep Jesus Christ, our God and our Lord, present within me.... [M]y imagination is so dull that I never succeeded even to think about and represent in my mind—as hard as I tried—the humanity of the Lord."[1] She struggled with her prayer life for eighteen years, even admitting, "I was more anxious that the hour I had determined to spend in prayer be over than I was to remain there, and more anxious to listen for the striking of the clock than to attend to other good things."[2] At the age of thirty-eight, her prayer life was uneventful until she experienced the image of "the sorely wounded Christ." About the same time, she was reading the *Confessions* of Saint Augustine and experienced profound feelings of repentance, receiving the gift of tears and consolation. Her prayer experiences intensified as she gave up control of her spiritual life and, with childlike trust and surrender, placed everything in God's hands.

Even her distractions no longer bothered her. She writes,

> Prayer is an act of love, words are not needed. Even if sickness distracts from thoughts, all that is needed is the will to love….
>
> [M]ental prayer in my opinion is nothing else than an intimate sharing between friends; it means taking time frequently to be alone with him who we know loves us. The important thing is not to think much but to love much and so do that which best stirs you to love. Love is not great delight but desire to please God in everything.[3]

Mystical experiences came in succession. Not yet conversant with the subtle stages of prayer and mystical experience, she hardly knew how to deal with them and sought advice from several spiritual directors. It was the time of the Inquisition, and while some directors thought she was faking it, others believed she was possessed by demonic forces.

The saintly Father Peter of Alcantara, however, understood her situation. Referring to his own personal experience, he explained to Teresa how God was working in her life. Other spiritual directors and confessors who were helpful in directing her included Saint Francis Borgia, Dominicans Pedro Ibañez and Domingo Bañez, the Jesuit priest Diego de Cetina and some seculars. Later, Teresa analyzed the stages of mystical experience in her autobiography (1565), in the *Way of Perfection*, and in what is considered to be one of the finest treatises on mystical theology, *The Interior Castle* (1583).

In her autobiography, Teresa divided prayer in four degrees or stages. Comparing the experience to tending a garden, the first stage of prayer (meditation) involves the hard work of fetching water from a distant well and carrying it in a bucket to water the garden. The second stage (prayer of recollection and quiet) involves the use of "a water wheel and aqueducts" as the individual begins to experience both active and passive prayers. The third stage (contemplation) is irrigation of the garden from "a river or a stream. The garden is watered much better by this means…much less work for the gardener." The fourth stage (prayer of union) is when it rains and "the Lord waters the garden without any work on our part...."[4]

Concerned about the superficial state of spirituality in many convents, she decided to bring the Carmelite Order back to its original roots and dedication to prayer, calling the reformed community Discalced (shoeless) Carmelites. In the face of intense, often savage, opposition, Teresa was eventually successful in establishing the convent of Discalced Carmelite Nuns of the Primitive Rule of Saint Joseph at Avila on August 24, 1562.

Teresa was denounced from the pulpit even as legal proceedings were brought against her. To top it all, she was reported to the Inquisition. In *The Long Loneliness: The Autobiography of Dorothy Day*, Day recounts a story she heard about Teresa that highlights some of the saint's humor and mettle in the midst of those harrowing times. Once when traveling with some nuns and priests, she had to cross a stream and was tossed from the donkey she was riding upon. She cried out to the Lord and asked why he done such a thing and she claims that he said, "That is how I treat my friends," to which Teresa dryly responded, "And that is why you have so few of them."[5]

Despite innumerable hardships and relentless opposition, Teresa established eighteen convents from 1567–1570. With the help of her friend and spiritual director, Saint John of the Cross, she also reformed the Carmelite friars, establishing several monasteries.

Teresa tirelessly encouraged her nuns to work and pray and never give in to physical or spiritual difficulties. In a letter she left for her spiritual daughters, she pointed out: "Remember you have only one soul; that you have one death to die; that you have only one life, which is short and has to be lived by you alone; and that there is only one glory, which is eternal. If you do this, there will be many things about which you care nothing."[6]

Teresa died in Alba de Tormes on October 4, 1582, at the age of sixty-seven. Her body has remained incorrupt and is kept in Alba, where it is venerated. Teresa was beatified on April 24, 1614, by Pope Paul V. In 1617, the Spanish parliament named her the patroness of Spain. Teresa was canonized, together with Ignatius of Loyola, Francis Xavier, Isidore and Philip Neri in 1622 by Pope Gregory XV. In 1970 she was declared a doctor of the church. With saint Thérèse of Lisieux and Catherine of Siena, Saint Teresa of Avila is one of only three female doctors of the Catholic church.[7]

Pope John XXIII

(1881–1963)

"There are three ways of ruining oneself—women, gambling, and farming. My father chose the most boring."[8]

—POPE JOHN XXIII

The fourth child in a family of humble peasants, the future Pope John XXIII, Angelo Giuseppe Roncalli, was born in Sotto il Monte, Italy, on November 25, 1881.

He entered the seminary in Bergamo in 1892. Three years later, as a fourteen-year-old seminarian, he wrote the first entry in what would become *Journal of a Soul*, a private diary which he kept faithfully throughout his life, filling up thirty-eight notebooks and folders. It was published in 1964, a year after his death.

He was admitted to the Secular Franciscan Order in 1897 and was ordained in 1904 in the church of Santa Maria in Monte Santo in Rome. When World War I broke out a decade later, Angelo was drafted into the Italian army and served as chaplain in the medical corps. His military experience made him a tireless advocate for peace among nations. His most famous encyclical was *"Pacem in Terris"* ("Peace on Earth"), written in 1963 and addressed not only to the Catholic church but to "all men of good will." Quoting Pope Pius XII, he wrote: "Nothing is lost by peace; everything is lost by war."[9]

Consecrated a bishop in 1925 by Pope Pius XI, he chose as his episcopal motto *Obedientia et Pax* (Obedience and Peace). After a diplomatic stint in Bulgaria as emissary of Pope Pius XI, Bishop Roncalli was appointed apostolic delegate to Turkey and Greece in 1935. Arriving in Istanbul as an unwanted person without diplomatic standing, he initiated dialogue with the Orthodox and Islamic religious communities there. Subjecting himself and his clergy to a government edict banning religious habits, he complied by surrendering his cassock, stating, "If in Rome Christ is a Roman, let him be a Turk in Turkey."[10]

Bishop Roncalli's open and conciliatory attitude showed the Turkish government the positive value of interfaith dialogue. In effect, he also safeguarded the fledgling Catholic population from government intrusion. Some of the Catholic faithful were unhappy when Roncalli read parts of the gospel and delivered his sermons in Turkish. But he was convinced that Catholicism must be universal and encompassing, rather than restrictive. As apostolic delegate, he also helped the Jewish underground movement save thousands of refugees by issuing "transit visas" from his office.

In 1944, Pope Pius XII appointed Roncalli apostolic nuncio to Paris, France. He was elevated to the office of cardinal and appointed patriarch of Venice in 1953. "The sense of my unworthiness keeps me good company," he said about his promotions in the hierarchy.[11]

To his surprise, the cheerful and witty Cardinal Roncalli was elected the pope on October 28, 1958, following the death of Pope Pius XII, which prompted him to say: "Anybody can be pope; the proof of this is that I have become one."[12] The conclave was looking for a transitional pope and considered Cardinal Roncalli a "safe" choice, because they assumed he would not rock the boat and make too many changes. Little did the College of Cardinals expect that Pope John's jovial personality, humor, kindness and charisma would captivate the world. His first official trip outside of the Vatican was to a prison where he addressed a gathering of amused inmates: "You could not come to see me, so I have come to see you!"[13]

Three months after his election to the papacy, and barely a century after Vatican Council I, Pope John XXIII stunned the Roman curia and the rest of the world when he called for an ecumenical council, commissioned to "opening the windows of the church" to the winds of change and the Holy Spirit. Indeed, Vatican Council II ushered the Catholic church into the modern era, catalyzing in the process the most profound restructuring of the church in four centuries.

Vatican II reevaluated the church's mission in the temporal world. It focused on social injustice and called for the "preferential option for the poor," out of which liberation theology was born. Inroads opened into ecumenism and inter-religious dialogue, into the promotion of global peace and the restructuring of society based on equality and justice. Vatican II changed the celebration of the Mass, introducing vernacular language, folk songs and local culture into the liturgical and sacramental life of the church. Church hierarchy and leadership were redirected toward the promotion of episcopal collegiality, a more pastoral clergy, and expanded roles for laypeople. The regal vestiges of the papacy were shed.

How such a simple, humble and self-effacing individual wrought so many changes to the modern church is remarkable. But perhaps not. Pope John XXIII once remarked:

> Everyone calls me "Holy Father," and holy I must and will be... [But] I am very far from attaining this holiness in fact , although my desire and will to succeed in this are whole-hearted and determined.... [S]anctity consists in being willing to be opposed and humiliated, rightly or wrongly; in being willing to obey;

in being willing to wait, with perfect serenity; in doing the will of your Superiors without regard for your own will; in acknowledging all the benefits you receive and your own unworthiness; in feeling a great gratitude to others....[14]

Pope John XXIII died on June 3, 1963, at age eighty-one of gastric cancer, unable to witness, but cognizant of the many fruits of Vatican II. He was posthumously awarded the Presidential Medal of Freedom, the United States' highest civilian award in December 1963. Many Protestant churches, including the Anglican and Lutheran churches, honor him as an important Christian reformer.

"Good Pope John" was beatified by Pope John Paul II in 2000. His body was transferred from its tomb below St. Peter's Basilica and placed near the main altar for public veneration. Blessed John XXIII's body is well preserved and appears incorruptible.

QUESTIONS FOR REFLECTION

1. What plan do you think God has in store for you? Has there been a time in your life where you have not understood God's plan? When you questioned God's love for you?

2. Can you trust God if you have no idea where you were going? Have you ever done that before?

SPIRITUAL EXERCISE

In our sufferings, difficulties, disappointments, when we feel lost and abandoned like the bamboo tree, we often question God's intention or ask the ever-frustrating "Why?" "Why me?" Find a space in your office or home sometime today, and sit silently and pray. Lay all your burdens and worries at the foot of the cross. Don't question anything for some time. But if you must ask God a question, instead of asking "Why?" try asking "Why not me?" or, "If not me, then who?" The answers might surprise you.

PRAYER

The Prayer of Abandonment of Brother Charles of Jesus

Father, I abandon myself into Your hands;

do with me what You will.

Whatever You do I thank You.

I am ready for all, I accept all.

Let only Your will be done in me,

as in all Your creatures,

I ask no more than this, my Lord.

Into Your hands I commend my soul;

I offer it to You, O Lord,

with all the love of my heart,

for I love You, my God, and so need to give myself—

to surrender myself into Your hands,

without reserve and with total confidence,

for You are my Father.[15]

—Charles de Foucauld

notes

[1] Kieran Kavanaugh, O.C.D., and Otilio Rodriguez, O.C.D., trans., *The Collected Works of St. Teresa of Avila, volume 1,* (Washington, D.C.: ICS, 1987), pp. 67–68.

[2] Kavanaugh and Rodriquez, *The Collected Works of St. Teresa of Avila, volume 1,* pp. 97–98.

[3] Terry Matz, "St. Teresa of Avila: Doctor of the Church," available at Catholic Online, http://www.catholic.org.

[4] Kieran Kavanaugh, O.C.D. and Otilio Rodriguez, O.C.D., trans. *The Collected Works of Saint Teresa of Avila, volume 2.,* (Washington, D.C.: ICS, 1980), pp. 110–119.

[5] Dorothy Day, *The Long Loneliness: The Autobiography of Dorothy Day* (San Francisco: HarperSanFrancisco, 1997), p. 140.

[6] Matthew Kelly, "What are you willing to give your life for?," Catholic Destination.com, August 4, 2007.

[7] Benedict Zimmerman. "St. Teresa of Avila," New Advent: Catholic Encyclopedia, http://www.newadvent.org.

[8] Lawrence Elliott. *I Will Be Called John: A Biography of Pope John XXIII* (New York: E. P. Dutton, 1973), p. 15.

[9] Elliott, p. 311.

[10] Elliott, p. 131.

[11] James Martin, S.J., *My Life with the Saints* (Chicago: Loyola, 2006), p. 189.

[12] Martin, p. 197.

[13] Elliott, p. 271.

[14] Pope John XXIII, *Journal of a Soul,* Dorothy White, trans. (New York: Image, 1980), p. 303.

[15] Charles de Foucauld, "The Prayer of Abandonment of Brother Charles of Jesus," http://www.tcrnews2.com/ramirez.html.

twelve

THE ART OF NOT TAKING ONESELF SERIOUSLY

Sense of Humor and Down-to-Earth Practicality

"And whenever you fast, do not look dismal, like the hypocrites, for they disfigure their faces so as to show others that they are fasting."

—MATTHEW 6:16

It was the last day of the year, and I was seeing my last patient, a consult for lower abdominal pain. I wished it would not be another appendicitis. It had been a very long day; I could hardly take one more trip to the operating room. Fortunately I found out, as I flipped open the medical chart, that the patient was ninety-five years old (appendicitis is most common in people between fifteen and thirty years old).

I found the patient in bed, engrossed in reading the local paper. I said hello and immediately the paper went down. Behind it was an impish face and a pair of mischievous, intelligent eyes. "Hi, Mr. C." I introduced myself, "Your physician has asked me to examine you. I am a surgeon and he tells me you've been experiencing a lot of belly pain."

"Yes, doctor," he said. "But, it's much better now. I think I just had the runs."

"How old are you?" I asked.

"Ninety-five, but, I will be ninety-six next month!" he exclaimed with good cheer, like a twelve-year-old eager to advance his age.

After I had examined him and noted that, indeed, he did not have a "surgical abdomen" (a condition that needed an operation, such as a perforated ulcer or diverticular abscess), I asked him what the secret of his longevity was.

He must have been asked that same question frequently. As if on cue, he proceeded to give me a pithy lecture on being happy, on living well:

Never worry. Problems come and go. I have yet to encounter a problem that did not eventually resolve itself.

Do not be anxious. Rest your mind, your spirit, your heart. It is not enough to rest your body—you need to rest your mind and spirit and soul as well.

Read a lot. Be interested in the world and in what's happening around you.

Go to your room and savor the silence.

Pray.

If I took those lessons to heart, I would hold a key to the secret of longevity and happiness.

 VIRTUOUS HEALERS WHO EXEMPLIFED
A SENSE OF HUMOR AND A DOWN-TO-EARTH PRACTICALITY

Saint Philip Neri

(1515–1595)

Philip Romolo Neri (Filippo de Neri) was born in Florence on July 21, 1515. He was the youngest child of Francesco Neri, a lawyer, and Lucrezia Soldi. Philip was educated by the Dominican friars at San Marco monastery in Florence. He gratefully acknowledged, later in life, the valuable education he received from his teachers, particularly Zenobio de Medici and Servanzio Mini.

When he was sixteen, a fire destroyed his family's property. Philip was sent to his Uncle Romolo, a merchant in San Germano, so he could apprentice and secure a brighter future. Philip's jolly disposition and work ethic made such an impression on Romolo that the merchant, who had no children, planned on leaving everything he possessed to Philip. However, the future "Apostle of Rome" resolved to serve God fully and was concerned that worldly success and material possessions might prevent him from pursuing a spiritual vocation. Therefore, in 1533, he left San Germano for Rome. Living in a garret, earning little from part-time tutoring, Philip continued his studies, this time under the Augustinians. Visiting churches and catacombs and working to help the sick and the poor, Philip was gearing up for what would become his life's mission.

Rome, at the time, had deteriorated morally and spiritually. Thus, Philip took on the daunting task of reevangelizing the seat of Christendom. He had no set plans, had not written a theological treatise, and did not belong to a religious congregation. Philip simply stood at street corners and talked to people. He had such an engaging personality; he was so friendly, witty and humorous, that he quickly developed a network of friends and acquaintances.

In 1548, at the age of thirty-three, Philip established the confraternity of the Santissima Trinita de'Pellegrini e de'Convalescente, whose mission was to minister to the needs of the thousands of poor pilgrims and to care for recuperating patients recently discharged from hospitals.

In 1551, on the advice of his confessor, Philip studied for the priesthood. Immediately following his ordination, people flocked to his Masses and penitents formed long lines outside his confessional. He started taking people on walking tours, discussing spiritual topics while visiting the basilicas of Rome. These local pilgrimages became so popular that civilian and ecclesiastical authorities started suspecting Father Philip had another agenda.

Wary of getting entangled in politics, Father Philip entertained the idea of leaving Rome to work as a missionary in India. However, his confessor persuaded him that there was more important work for him to do in Rome. So, he continued his "home mission" and resided at the hospital of San Girolamo della Carita.

In 1556, Father Philip initiated a series of evening meetings in an oratory, a hall where people congregated to pray, to listen to readings from Scripture, the desert fathers and the lives of the saints and to sing sacred hymns and discuss relevant religious and theological issues. Laypeople were invited to preach in the meetings—a radical concept at that time. This novel program of evangelization, embellished with musical renditions (oratorios) of scenes from sacred history, became so successful that a new society was born, the Congregation of the Oratory.

In 1564, Father Philip was asked to be pastor of the newly constructed church of San Giovanni de Fiorentini but he was reluctant to leave San Girolamo and take on the new assignment. However, on the advice of Pope Pius IV, Father Philip accepted the new job while continuing to supervise the oratories at San Girolamo. His society flourished, attracting talented laity and clergy. Distinguished scholars, historians and future bishops and cardinals joined the popular congregation. One of the more famous members of his society was John Henry Newman who went on to establish the first oratories in London.

In 1574, the society's headquarters was transferred from San Girolamo hospital to San Giovanni church. As the congregation continued to grow even further, the main house was moved to the bigger church of Santa Maria. The Congregation of the Oratory, a community of secular priests, was formally organized by Father Philip with the approval of Pope Gregory XIII on July 15, 1575. The congregation spread rapidly in Italy and in France and, by 1760, it had grown to fifty-eight houses. He was elected superior for life of the community but, wary of assuming a position of authority, Father Philip decreed that congregations formed outside of Rome should be autonomous and self-governing. "If you want to be obeyed," he remarked, "don't give commands."

Healing miracles were attributed to Father Philip when he and his chaplains carried their missions through the hospitals in Rome. People regarded Father Philip as a living saint and noted that when he celebrated Mass, his face often shone with a supernatural glow, as he lapsed into ecstatic union.

Despite his celebrity status, Father Philip remained humble and down-to-earth. He frequently carried out practical jokes and occasionally dressed up in comical outfits. At times he would show up with only one side of his face shaved. He truly enjoyed making people laugh.

Following his death on May 26, 1595, the comical and beloved Father Philip Neri was beatified by Paul V in 1600, and canonized by Gregory XV in 1622.

Blessed Artemide Zatti
(1880–1951)

Artemide Zatti was born in Reggio Emilia, Italy on October 12, 1880. Seventeen years later, his family emigrated and settled in Bahía Blanca, Argentina. The Zatti family was actively involved in the local parish which was run by the Salesian fathers. Working in a hotel and, later, in a brick factory, Artemide found time to help the Salesian priests with parochial projects, particularly visiting and attending to the sick.

There he learned of Saint John Bosco, founder of the Salesians. Inspired to imitate the saint, Artemide entered the Salesian Order, at age nineteen, to study for the priesthood. However, having been out of school for some time, he struggled academically. Attending to TB patients, he also contracted tuberculosis. Thus, he left the seminary in 1902 to reside temporarily in Viedma, a city situated up in the Andes, where the cool, clean air was thought to be therapeutic.

In Viedma, the Salesian college had a pharmacy and St. Joseph of the Mission, a seventy-bed hospital managed by a physician-priest, Father Evaristo Garrone. No patient was ever turned away from the facility because Father Garrone's strict rule was that "[the patient] who has little, pays little and the one who has nothing pays nothing."[1]

With Father Garrone's guidance, Artemide became a Salesian religious brother in 1908. He had been cured of his TB through the intercession of Our Lady Help of Christians, to whom Artemide had fervently prayed, vowing he would spend the rest of his life serving the poor and the sick.

Artemide worked closely with Father Garrone and when the physician-priest died in 1911, Artemide took over the management of the pharmacy and the hospital. In this capacity, he wore many hats as trained pharmacist, nurse, operating-room assistant, bookkeeper and CEO of sorts. Following Father Garrone's rule and trusting completely in divine providence, Artemide ran the Salesian hospital and pharmacy successfully for the next forty years.

It was remarkable how Artemide carried on his dual role as a religious brother, with responsibilities to the Salesian community, and as a hospital administrator and pharmacist, attending daily to inpatients and outpatients. Despite the demands and stresses of his job, he was not known to complain. On the contrary, he was admired for his "Salesian joy." Artemide inspired patients and hospital staff with his sanctity; many would say that "was he not only provider of medicine, but was himself a medicine for others by his presence, his songs, his voice...."[2]

In July 1950, Artemide sustained serious injuries from falling off a ladder while fixing a leaky water tank and was hospitalized. Coincidentally, he was found to be jaundiced and diagnosed with liver cancer. However,

Artemide's humor and cheerfulness never left him even when terminally ill, referring in jest to the tumor as a cantaloupe he had to carry. He died on March 15, 1951 and was buried in the chapel of the Salesians at Viedma, Argentina. He was eventually declared blessed by Pope John Paul II.

QUESTIONS FOR REFLECTIONS

1. Do you take yourself too seriously? Is everything a big deal to you?
2. Are people uptight when they are near you? Do you make people uncomfortable?
3. Can you laugh at your mistakes?

SPIRITUAL EXERCISE

Look at a single embarrassing episode in your life. Can you laugh at it now? If not at first, why? What do you think you need to do to laugh at yourself?

PRAYER

Lord, I am going to bed…

It's your turn now to take care of the world.

—Evening prayer attributed to Pope John XXIII

notes

[1] "Artemide Zatti," available at www.vatican.va.

[2] "Artemide Zatti."

thirteen

THE CONSUMMATE PHYSICIAN
Science and Religion, Technology and Spirituality, Academics and Faith

"I do not call you servants any longer, because the servant does not know what the master is doing; but I have called you friends, because I have made known to you everything that I have heard from my Father. You did not choose me but I chose you. And I appointed you to go and bear fruit, fruit that will last, so that the Father will give you whatever you ask him in my name. I am giving you these commands so that you may love one another."

—JOHN 15:15–17

One of the most beloved geniuses of our time, Albert Einstein, said: "Science without religion is lame; religion without science is blind."

Just as science, devoid of faith and religion, is sterile, spirituality in medicine, detached from science, borders on "faith healing." If we do not allow the spiritual dimension of our medical work to flourish, we turn into one-dimensional "medi-robots." In like manner, our treatment can endanger our patients' health if based on patchy scientific data.

I recall the unfortunate case of a priest who went on a pilgrimage and was so touched by his religious experience that he stopped taking his cardiac medications, confident that he had been divinely healed. A few months after shelving his medicines, he developed irreversible cardiac failure and died.

If patients were asked who they would prefer to perform surgery on them: unsympathetic but competent doctors or technically incompetent surgeons who can pray with them, we can guess what their choice would be. The ideal, of course, is to have both scientific and religious dimensions in a complete physician.

Our times are marked by a relentless focus on continuing medical education and cutting-edge science, which is well and good, if spirituality, idealism and humanism are not left abandoned by the wayside. In medicine, as in many other endeavors, it is worthwhile to aim for balance.

VIRTUOUS HEALERS WHO EXEMPLIFIED
FINDING THE BALANCE BETWEEN SCIENCE AND RELIGION,
TECHNOLOGY AND SPIRITUALITY, ACADEMICS AND FAITH

Pierre Teilhard de Chardin

(1881–1955)

Pierre Teilhard de Chardin was born on May 1, 1881, in the Auvergne region of France. He inherited his scientific aptitude from his naturalist father and his spirituality from his religious mother. He attended the Jesuit college of Mongré, in Villefranche-sur-Saône, and became a Jesuit novitiate at Aix-en-Provence in 1899, at the age of eighteen. Completing double baccalaureates in philosophy and mathematics, he also earned a licentiate in literature.

As a Jesuit scholastic he taught physics and chemistry at the Jesuit College of the Holy Family in Cairo, Egypt, then studied theology in Hastings, Sussex. As he pursued his interest and research in geology and paleontology, he began synthesizing his scientific findings with philosophy and theology. Teilhard was ordained to the priesthood on August 24, 1911, at the age of thirty.

A year after ordination, he worked at the Museum of Natural History in Paris until December 1914, when he was drafted to serve as a stretcher-bearer, receiving the Médaille Militaire and the Legion of Honor for valiant service. While in the military, he penned his reflections in journals and in letters to his cousin Marguerite Teillard-Chambon, who collected them in a book, *Genesis of a Thought*. In 1916, he wrote his first essay, "Cosmic Life," which bridged his scientific and theological thinking. In August 1919, he wrote *The Spiritual Power of Matter* and lectured in geology at the Catholic Institute of Paris, becoming an assistant professor after earning a doctorate there.

In explaining the teleological unfolding of the universe in scientific and theological language, Teilhard metaphorically interpreted the book of Genesis, which did not sit well with some members of the Roman curia. Teilhard viewed the cosmos as the progressive evolution of matter and energy—inanimate matter evolved into cellular forms of life which in turn evolved into more complex organisms. He theorized that, as evolution continued, human consciousness will ascend to such sublime levels that a "noosphere" (or cosmic consciousness) will inevitably develop. Ultimately, the highest transformation of spirit and matter will converge in "Omega Point," the summit of which is consummated in Jesus Christ.

Teilhard was not formally condemned by the Vatican but his superiors forbade him from disseminating his theological ideas through publications or lectures. In 1925, the Jesuit superior general ordered Teilhard to relinquish his position at the Catholic Institute and to sign a statement withdrawing his statements on the doctrine of original sin. Teilhard signed the statement and was "exiled" to China.

This was frustrating and painful for Teilhard—he could not deny and abandon his scientific theories nor could he leave the Jesuit Order, much less the Catholic church to which in conscience he remained faithful—thus, in the spirit of obedience he left for China in April 1926. He would remain there for two decades as part of the team which in December 1929 discovered *Sinanthropus pekinensis* or Peking Man, the nearest kin of *Pithecanthropus* from Java. Thereafter, Teilhard wrote *The Spirit of the Earth*. He also created the first general geological map of China.

In 1937 Teilhard wrote *The Spiritual Phenomenon* onboard the *Empress of Japan* on the way to the United States, where he was awarded the Mendel medal at Villanova University in recognition of his contribution to human palaeontology. Recuperating from malaria, he wrote *Spiritual Energy of Suffering*. Teilhard died of a heart attack on April 10, 1955, in New York City on Easter Sunday. He was buried at the Jesuit seminary at Saint Andrews-on-Hudson.

Teilhard de Chardin's problems with the Vatican continued beyond his death. But as time passed, his once-controversial ideas gradually gained favor. In science and technology, the far-reaching ideas of Teilhard de Chardin inspired Silicon Valley engineers working on the integrated chip. While the Internet is a rather primitive form of Teilhard's "noosphere," it is fascinating to think how a brilliant Jesuit priest who studied fossils as an avocation foresaw the future of technology and science, when he wrote:

> Among so many great events, there is one phenomenon which, in the eyes of posterity, may well overshadow everything that has been discovered in radiation and electricity: the permanent entry into operation, in our day, of inter-human affinities—the movement, irresistible and ever increasing in speed, which we can see for ourselves, welding peoples and individuals to another....[1]

Teilhard's vision did not stop here. "The day will come," he wrote, "when, after harnessing space, the winds, the tides, gravitation, we shall harness for God the energies of love. And, on that day, for the second time in the history of the world, man will have discovered fire."[2]

Doctor Alexis Carrel

(1 8 7 3 – 1 9 4 4)

Alexis was born on June 28, 1873, in Sainte-Foy-les-Lyon, France. Raised in a Catholic home with two brothers and a sister, Alexis was educated by the Jesuits. He entered medical school at the University of Lyons in 1891, after earning two baccalaureate degrees in letters and in science.

After a hospital internship and serving a year as an army surgeon, he lectured and conducted research at the University of Lyons, hoping to earn a tenured faculty position. He was initially interested in finding a way to repair and suture blood vessels together as he was convinced that the president of France would not have bled to death had arterial repair been possible. Experimenting with fine needles and silk thread and testing out various techniques, Doctor Carrel successfully connected an artery (a procedure known as anastomosis) and published his findings in a French medical journal in 1902.

Despite his success as a surgical researcher, Doctor Carrel was not given tenure in the university. His peers were unimpressed with his research and Doctor Carrel, in turn, was critical of the medical status quo. The final straw came when Doctor Carrel, after a pilgrimage to Lourdes, wrote a favorable piece about the miraculous healings occurring at the Marian shrine, in which he intimated that scientific investigation of religious phenomena may be worthwhile. That position drew sharp criticism from both the scientific and clerical establishments.

In June 1904, Doctor Carrel left France for Montreal, Canada. His conversations with French missionaries posted in Canada had influenced his decision to explore the possibility of working there. But, Doctor Carrel was offered a position at the Hull Physiology Laboratory of the

University of Chicago, so he worked there instead for two years, continuing his research on vascular techniques, blood transfusion and organ transplantation. Doctor Carrel performed kidney transplants in canine models and his groundbreaking work, which envisioned the possibility of human organ transplant, drew the attention of scientists and the media.

In 1906, Doctor Carrel was given the opportunity to work at the new Rockefeller Institute for Medical Research in New York City. Focused entirely on medical research, the Rockefeller Institute was the first of its kind in the United States. Doctor Carrel would remain at the Institute for the next thirty-three years, continuing his pioneering work in vascular surgery, blood coagulation, storage and transfusion.

In 1910, he wrote an article in the *Journal of the American Medical Association* (JAMA) where he described anastomosing an artery from the arm of a father to the leg of an infant to replace blood lost from intestinal bleeding. In 1912, Doctor Carrel became the first scientist in the United States to receive the Nobel Prize in medicine and physiology for his pioneering work on vascular surgery and animal organ transplantation. Doctor Carrel's work on tissue cultures and organ perfusion also helped advance the research in virology and the preparation of vaccines.

Doctor Carrel was as devoted to science as he was to his faith. While working in the United States, Carrel made a pilgrimage to Lourdes each August. On December 26, 1913, Carrel married Anne-Marie Laure de Meyrie, whom he had met at Lourdes. He died in 1944.

QUESTIONS FOR REFLECTION

1. Have you kept up with the latest advances in your field?
2. Have you been too busy or too comfortable with scientific knowledge that may be antiquated?
3. In your early career, you may have leaned toward scientific reading. Later in life, as you progressed in the spiritual journey, your preference may have shifted to books about faith, religion and spirituality.

Remember what Saint Thomas Aquinas said: "*In medio stat virtus.*" ("Virtue is in the middle ground.") Continue to read both and nourish your intellect as well as your soul.

SPIRITUAL EXERCISE

In the future for every spiritual book that you read, pick up and read a scientific journal. And for every journal that you read, pick up and read a spiritual book.

PRAYER

Thy will be done on earth
As it is in heaven...

notes

1 Pierre Teilhard de Chardin, *Toward the Future* (London: Collins, 1975), pp. 86–87.

2 Teilhard de Chardin, pp. 86–87.

f o u r t e e n

NO-FRILLS MEDICINE

Social Justice and the Preferential Option for the Poor

> *"'…[f]or I was hungry and you gave me food, I was thirsty and you gave me something to drink, I was a stranger and you welcomed me, I was naked and you gave me clothing, I was sick and you took care of me, I was in prison and you visited me….' 'Truly I tell you, just as you did it to one of the least of these who are members of my family, you did it to me.'"*
>
> —MATTHEW 25: 35–36, 40

Can medicine be dispensed without monetary considerations? Can patients be treated for free? In the past, faith healers attended to the sick without compensation. Why can't modern doctors and nurses offer their services gratis?

In the practice of medicine, at least in the United States, nothing today is more problematic than service to the poor. Medicine in the twenty-first century has become technologically complex and dependent on increasingly expensive drugs and machines. Having evolved into a billion-dollar industry, economics have essentially dominated the equation and the poor have been left out of the picture.

The federal government has grappled with the issue at length yet practically half of today's patient population, in many regions in the United States, are either medically uninsured or on state or federal assistance. Medicare's progressively reduced reimbursements have in turn emboldened private insurance carriers to copy the federal government program's decreasing rates, in effect shifting the economic burden of healthcare to physicians and hospitals.

On the other end of the equation, the costs of medical education and training, maintaining professional certification and continuing medical education have skyrocketed. The days of simply hanging out a shingle are over. Young physicians, carrying over enormous educational debts from medical school, become business-oriented as they quickly find out that maintaining a viable practice entails the expense of staffing, furnishing and stocking an office. Most are unprepared as they confront the non-medical complexities of taxes, payrolls, regulatory requirements—in essence, running a small business. Put these financially strapped new graduates into a mix of long hours and short pay and something is bound to break, idealism and altruism notwithstanding.

The general public has yet to fully grasp the implications of financially burdened medical practitioners. Doctors, in the public eye, are an educated and privileged class. Surely, a few pay cuts will not jeopardize their lifestyles. Yet, if the trend continues, it will become more and more difficult to attract the best and the brightest to the practice of medicine.

Idealism and service to humanity may compel a few selfless individuals to go through the rigors of medical education and training but, in today's setting, these may not be enough to sustain a steady influx of dedicated and knowledgeable physicians.

As medicine has become more complex, clinical errors have increased and malpractice claims have flourished. Increasing malpractice insurance costs and overhead expenses financially squeeze physicians to the point where they feel shortchanged or, at least, like they are shouldering more than their share of pro bono work. Why provide free care when it is difficult enough to keep the doors open treating insured and paying patients?

Social justice, if anything, means just wages and sufficient compensation for labor expended and services rendered. One's work, theoretically, should not only cover work-related expenses but provide the means to support a family and educate the children. The tricky part is: How much is one's work worth? What is just compensation? How much can one ethically draw from society's goods for one's own benefit, without unjustly subtracting from one's neighbor?

It is encouraging that many physicians still go out of their way to extend high quality medical services to the poor in their communities and, in some cases, to those beyond their borders. Physicians are, for the most part, charitable at heart, born with a sensitivity radar for the needs (at least the physical needs) of fellow human beings. Many of us still hold to the truth that our character, our integrity, our legacy are measured in the way we treat the poor, the widow, the orphan—our brothers and sisters, children of God, who have missed out on society's blessings and opportunities.

What is the answer to this problem? Is it universal healthcare, medical savings accounts, government-sponsored hospitals, subsidized physicians? Is the solution a two-tiered system—one for those who can afford to pay for medical care and another for those who cannot? Global insurance? Is the solution to create more charity clinics, more federally funded healthcare facilities? To create and organize more paramedical forces—nurse practitioners, physician assistants, alternative health practitioners?

Encountering such problems, what would the saints have done? We read of Saint Martin of Tours tearing his cloak in half when he met a naked beggar. We read of Artimide Zatti trusting that divine providence was infinitely rich enough to provide care to all patients. We read of Saint Alphonsus Liguori encouraging us to care for the sick who, after all, depend on us for help. We read of Mother Teresa of Calcutta who tells us to not count the cost, but to give everything of ourselves.

One remarkable nun I know trained in a surgical residency program, late in her career, so she could meet the needs of the poor in her community. But surgeon nuns are rare—I've met only two. Surely, they can be our models. Selfless, dedicated, not counting the cost, while ministering to the sickest and the poorest—these saintly nuns are the worthy heirs of Hippocrates.

But, how many can or will follow their path?

VIRTUOUS HEALERS WHO EXEMPLIFED
SOCIAL JUSTICE AND PREFERENTIAL OPTION FOR THE POOR

Blessed Damien of Molokai
(1840–1889)

Damien of Molokai was selfless, dedicated and passionate about taking care of the poorest and the sickest lepers. Born on January 3, 1840, to Frans and Anne Catherine de Veuster, Joseph, or Jef—(he changed his name to Damien when he entered religious life, in honor of an ancient physician-saint)—grew up in the village of Tremeloo, near the city of Louvain in Belgium. The Flemish family of eight siblings was blessed with religious vocations—sisters Eugenie and Pauline became Ursuline nuns and brother Auguste joined the Congregation of the Sacred Hearts of Jesus and Mary—partly as a result of Anne Catherine's religious instructions. She owned an impressive Old Flemish volume about the lives of martyrs, hermits and saints, from which she often read to her children.

On February 2, 1859, Jef was admitted to the order of the Congregation of the Sacred Hearts Fathers, as was his older brother

Auguste (Father Pamphile) before him. He was assigned the position of choir brother to attend to the chapel and infirmarian to nurse the sick and the elderly.

Damien's older brother, Father Pamphile, was scheduled to leave for the Sandwich Islands (now Hawaii) as a missionary but was struck down with typhus fever. Brother Damien requested and received permission to take Father Pamphile's place. On October 20, 1863, the twenty-three-year-old Damien joined other missionaries and after 148 days at sea on board the merchant ship *R.M. Wood*, they arrived at the port of Honolulu.

Brother Damien continued his theological studies at the missions college in Ahuimanu and was ordained to the priesthood. On May 21, 1864, Father Damien de Veuster, SS.CC. celebrated his first Mass at the Cathedral of Our Lady of Peace in Honolulu.

Eager to start his missionary work, Father Damien set sail for the big island of Hawaii where he would spend eight years in intensive pastoral work. Legend has it that he visited far-flung parishioners on horseback and that he built with his bare hands many of the chapels and small churches around the big island.

When Father Damien learned that hundreds of lepers were being quarantined on the island of Molokai without anyone regularly ministering to their physical and spiritual needs, he requested to be transferred to the island. On May 10, 1873, Father Damien, age thirty-three, with only his crucifix, a breviary and the clothes on his back, left Kohala on the big island and, with Bishop Louis Maigret, superior of the Sacred Hearts Congregation in the Sandwich Islands, arrived at his new parish in Kalawao, Molokai, at about the time when the Norwegian Gerhard Henrick Armauer Hansen had successfully identified *Bacillus leprae*, the causative agent for leprosy (Hansen's disease). Hansen's groundbreaking scientific work paved the way for identifying, isolating and ultimately controlling such deadly diseases as tuberculosis, typhoid fever, syphilis and diphtheria. But leprosy, an affliction well known since biblical times, would remain infectious and incurable for some time.

Undeterred by the dangers of close contact with lepers, Father Damien ministered to the settlement and wrote to his superiors that he wished to be assigned permanently to the Kalaupapa Peninsula rather than rotating with other priest volunteers. On the big island, he had honed his farming and carpentry skills. Consumed with the desire to alleviate the pain and suffering of the nearly eight-hundred leprosy patients scattered throughout the island of Molokai, Father Damien also became a sort of medicine man.

In November 1883, Mother Marianne Cope with six other sisters of the Third Order of Saint Francis from Syracuse, New York, arrived in Hawaii. They worked at the leprosy receiving facility in Kakaako, Oahu, for five years before transferring to Kalaupapa on November 14, 1888, to assist Father Damien and manage the Bishop Home for Girls. Mother Marianne came to Molokai on a steamer with forty-two patients. She quickly instituted sanitation practices to protect her healthcare workers from contracting the disease. As administrator, educator and nurse, Mother Marianne effected many positive changes in the leper colony until her death twenty-nine years later on August 9, 1918. In 1884, directed by the Board of Health, Doctor Arthur Mouritz from Germany moved into the settlement to provide full-time medical services.

On March 30, 1886, Father Damien was diagnosed with Hansen's disease, yet, he continued his daily work routine. There was much work to do as the number of patients in the settlement had reached a thousand. On April 15, 1889, the first day of Holy Week, at the age of forty-nine, febrile, covered with leprosy sores, crippled and suffering, Father Damien passed away. At the Kalaupapa National Historical Park, Damien's words are inscribed: "I am gently going to my grave. It is the will of God and I thank Him very much for letting me die of the same disease and in the same way as my lepers. I am very satisfied and very happy."

On July 7, 1977, Pope Paul VI declared Father Damien venerable and on June 4, 1995, he was beatified by Pope John Paul II at the Koelkelberg Basilica in Brussels. Pope John Paul II also declared May 10, the day Father Damien arrived in Molokai, as Blessed Damien's feast day. King Albert II of Belgium and Mother Teresa of Calcutta, longtime admirers of Father Damien, were among the twenty-five thousand in attendance at the beatification ceremony, as were a number of patients from Kalaupapa.

Dorothy Day

(1897–1980)

A young rebel, a temperamental Bohemian, a brilliant journalist, an incarcerated political protester, an avowed pacifist, a courageous advocate for the poor and the homeless, a compassionate nurse, a devoutly practicing Catholic—in whatever category one puts her, the consensus is that Dorothy Day is an interesting, if controversial, twentieth-century firebrand who lived the gospel of Jesus Christ to the letter. Like Saint Francis of Assisi before her, she read Matthew 25 and followed its precepts literally. Such heroic living of Christ's teachings makes Dorothy Day a powerful, compelling and inspiring Christian model for all ages.

Dorothy was born in Brooklyn, New York, on November 8, 1897, and baptized in an Episcopalian church. Her father was a journalist from Tennessee. Her paternal grandfather, Doctor Sam Houston Day, was a surgeon who served in the Confederate Army. In Bath Beach, Brooklyn, where Dorothy grew up, she did not recall going to church with her two brothers and sister. The family instead spent weekends on the beach, playing and fishing. The family moved to California later when Dorothy was about eight, then moved back east to Chicago. Despite the relocations, Dorothy recalled having a happy childhood.

In her teen years, Dorothy was a voracious reader and well informed in history and politics. At the University of Illinois, she joined the Socialist Party, appalled at "the ugliness of life in a world which professed itself to be Christian...." The Marxist slogan "Workers of the world, unite! You have nothing to lose but your chains" appealed to her idealism. But even as she veered from organized religion, the Russian authors Dostoevsky and Tolstoy "made me cling to a faith in God."[1] Dorothy often quoted the wise monk Father Zossima from Dostoevsky's novel, *The Brothers Karamazov*. Responding to a wealthy lady's musings about dedicating her life to the service of poor, but held back by their ingratitude, Father Zossima remarked: "Love in practice is a hard and dreadful thing compared to love in dreams."[2]

Dorothy realized the need for charitable projects but also questioned the socioeconomic status quo which kept the poor from improving their condition. "Where were the saints to try to change the social order, not just to minister to the slaves but to do away with slavery?" she asked.[3]

In the summer of 1916, Dorothy's father was offered a desk job with the *Morning Telegraph* in New York and relocated his family once more. Dorothy got her first job in New York, writing for the socialist paper, the *New York Call*. She covered radical meetings, protest marches, picket lines and strikes. She associated with liberals and radicals and picketed the White House with the suffragists. Her political activities landed her in jail, where she participated in a hunger strike.

In 1918, unhappy with the absence of direction in her life, Dorothy became a student nurse at Kings County Hospital in Brooklyn. She was a pacifist, viewing warfare as nothing less than murder, but understood the need to take care of wounded soldiers. The influenza epidemic was also raging and she was "heart-broken to see young people dying all around us of the flu."

Excerpts of Dorothy Day's letters to her brother and in her autobiography offer insight into nursing care during her time and to her growing attraction to religion. She had long days and endured hours of intense physical labor, but still managed to go to Mass every day. [5]

After a year, Dorothy "felt that nursing was not my vocation and that my real work was writing and propaganda...."[6] She left Kings County hospital and pursued journalism. A friend persuaded her to buy a house on the beach in Staten Island, where she could settle down to serious writing, which she did after the movie rights to her memoir sold for five-thousand dollars. Later, in her autobiography, she wrote that "[I]f I had not had the irresistible urge to write, I would have clung to the profession of nursing as the most noble work [I] could aspire to."[7]

Dorothy settled down, had a baby girl, Tamar Teresa (named after Saint Teresa of Avila), attended Sunday Mass regularly and started reading Scripture, the Imitation of Christ, and the works of Saint Teresa and Saint John of the Cross.

After much soul-searching, Dorothy had Tamar Teresa baptized as a Roman Catholic. In 1927, at the age of thirty-one, she herself was baptized conditionally (she had already been baptized as an Episcopalian), made her first confession and received Holy Communion. She terminated her common-law marriage and began to live a radically authentic Christian life. On the difficulty of living a truly Christian life, she would say: "Christ [is] not to be bought for thirty pieces of silver but with my heart's blood."[8]

In 1932, she met Peter Maurin, with whom she cofounded the Catholic Worker movement. They launched a paper which provided a common forum for poor and exploited workers, analyzing labor issues from the gospel's perspective. The inaugural issue of 2,500 copies was sold for one cent a copy on May 1, 1933. Its circulation quickly jumped to 25,000 and three years later to 150,000 copies. The paper still sells today for a penny a copy.

Constantly in financial straits, the Catholic Worker movement nevertheless flourished. The Catholic Worker houses in New York City, named after Saint Joseph and the Blessed Virgin Mary, attracted idealistic young men and women who volunteered to help shelter and feed the homeless, assist the unemployed, and organize retreats, conferences and political protests. These houses were quickly duplicated across the United States. "Do you have ecstasies and visions?" Dorothy was once asked, to which she replied, "Visions of unpaid bills."[9]

In one of the retreats I attended, the priest giving the conference said that he was a seminarian who was assigned, as part of his community service, to spend a Saturday morning visiting the local prison. He was instructed to meet with other students in front of a designated building but when he arrived, no one was there. Knocking on the front door and getting no response, he made his way to the back of the building and saw the cleaning lady working in the kitchen.

She was sweeping the floor when he tapped on the screen door and asked, "Excuse me, ma'am, but do you know if the students had already left for their prison assignment?" "Yes, they left a while ago," the old lady replied. "Do you know how to get there?" she asked him. He said no. "Well," she said, "if you wait a minute, I just need to finish cleaning up and I can go with you to the prison."

Her task done, she handed him a couple of bread baskets to carry and a key to the van in the garage. When they arrived at the prison compound, the seminarian asked if she would rather wait in the van. He was just going to deliver the bread quickly and leave. He was concerned that, as frail as she was, she might get hurt if a riot broke out. "No, don't worry," she assured him; she was going to be fine.

As soon as they entered, he thought they had walked into a riot! The prisoners were yelling and screaming as they came in. Except for the clueless seminarian, all the prisoners knew the old lady who frequently visited and attended to their needs. They all loved Dorothy Day.

Dorothy Day's cause for beatification was initially promoted by the late Archbishop of New York, Cardinal John O'Connor and continued by the present Archbishop Cardinal Edward Egan. Some contend that her beatification and canonization are long overdue. Yet, members of the Catholic Worker movement, prefer that the resources required to advance her beatification process are better spent for the care, feeding and sheltering of what was closest to Dorothy's heart—the urban poor. They recall that she often said: "When they call you a saint, it means basically that you're not to be taken seriously."[10] Like her favorite saint, Teresa of Avila, however, Dorothy Day did confess that in her younger days, "I was filled with lofty ambitions to be a saint, a natural striving, a thrilling recognition of the possibilities of spiritual adventure."[11]

Many who have admiringly followed her life and accomplishments would be happy to see Dorothy Day elevated to sainthood, though others feel that her early unconventional lifestyle makes her a controversial role model. All agree that Dorothy Day was passionate in her belief that all of God's children—meaning all of us—and not only a select few are called to holiness and should strive to become saints.

QUESTIONS FOR REFLECTION

1. How can you provide care to those who cannot afford medical care?
2. Can you see Christ in your poor patients?
3. Should you leave the care of the poor for the government to solve?
4. Can you open or work in clinics where the poor can be served?

SPIRITUAL EXERCISE

Sit quietly, take a few deep breaths, close your eyes. Transport yourself to your days of medical training. No, perhaps, farther back, when the idea of entering medicine, helping and caring for the sick, germinated in your brain, in your heart, in your soul. What were your goals then? Have your goals and priorities changed? Have you become less idealistic and more realistic?

PRAYER

Sacred Heart of Jesus and Immaculate Heart of Mary,
I offer myself totally to the Your Most Holy Love
I wish to make reparation for all my sins and of the whole world.

Help me keep my mind on goodness and beauty.
Help me bear the mistakes of others with love and a forgiving heart.
Help me to admit when I am wrong and ask others for forgiveness.
Help me not to seek rewards, but to seek the last place.

Help me to always follow God's Will.
Help me to appreciate the blessings I receive.
Help me to be grateful for everything.

I offer up all my trials and sufferings.
Let me fully trust in Divine Providence.
Let me love others, as God loves me.

Sacred Heart of Jesus,
through the intercession of the Immaculate Heart of Mary,
kindly receive the offering and consecration I make of myself.
Bring me one day to the happy home in heaven.
Amen.

notes

1 Dorothy Day, "From Union Square to Rome," *The Catholic Worker* available at at www.catholicworker.org/dorothyday.

2 Jim Forest, "Dorothy Day, Saint and Troublemaker," available at www.meetingground.org/loavfish/lf798/day.htm.

3 Day, "From Union Square to Rome."

4 Ellsberg, *All Saints*, p. 519.

5 Day, "From Union Square to Rome."

6 Day, "From Union Square to Rome."

7 Day, *The Long Loneliness*, p. 94.

8 Ellsberg, *All Saints*, p. 520.

9 Day, *The Long Loneliness*, p. 188.

10 Ellsberg, *All Saints*, p. 519.

11 Day, "From Union Square to Rome."

BIBLIOGRAPHY

Books

Allen, John L. *Opus Dei, An Objective Look Behind the Myths and Reality of the Most Controversial Force in the Catholic Church*. New York: Doubleday, 2005.

Balducci, Ernesto. *John : The Transitional Pope*. Dorothy White, trans. New York: McGraw-Hill, 1964.

Ball, Ann. *Modern Saints: Their Lives and Faces*. Rockford, Ill.: TAN, 1990.

Bernardin, Joseph. *The Gift of Peace*. Chicago: Loyola University Press, 1997.

Bonhoeffer, Dietrich. *The Cost of Discipleship*. New York: Touchstone, 1995.

_____. *Ethics*. New York: Touchstone, 1995.

_____. *Letters & Papers from Prison*. New York: Collier, 1972.

Brabazon, James. *Albert Schweitzer: A Biography*. New York: G.P. Putnam's Sons, 1975.

Brocker, James H., *The Land of Father Damien*. James H. Brocker, 1998.

Brockman, James R., *Romero: A Life*. Maryknoll, N.Y.: Orbis 1989.

Brother Lawrence of the Resurrection, *The Practice of the Presence of God*. John J. Delaney, trans. New York: Image Doubleday, 1977.

_____. *The Practice of the Presence of God*. Salvatore Sciurba, trans. Washington, D.C.: ICS, 1994.

Bunson, Margaret R., *Father Damien: The Man and His Era*. Huntington, Ind.: Our Sunday Visitor, 1997.

Chalika, Jaya and Edward Le Joly. *The Joy of Loving: Mother Teresa*. New York: Penguin, 2000.

Chesterton, G.K. *Orthodoxy*. San Francisco: Ignatius, 1995.

Collopy, Michael, *Works of Love are Works of Peace.* San Francisco: Ignatius, 1996.

Cuenot, Claude. *Science and Faith in Teilhard de Chardin.* London: Garnstone, 1967.

Daws, Gavan, *Holy Man: Father Damien of Molokai.* Honolulu, Hawaii: University of Hawaii Press, 1973.

Day, Dorothy. *The Long Loneliness.* New York: Harper and Row, 1952, 1980.

De Caussade, Jean-Pierre. *Abandonment to Divine Providence.* John Beevers, trans. New York: Image Doubleday, 1975.

De Chardin, Pierre Teilhard. *Human Energy.* New York: Harcourt Brace Jovanovich, 1971.

_____. *The Divine Milieu: An Essay on the Interior Life.* New York: Harper and Row, 1968.

_____. *The Future of Man.* Norman Denny, trans. New York: Harper and Row, 1964.

_____. *Toward the Future.* Rene Hague, trans. New York: Harcourt Brace Jovanonich, 1973.

_____. *Writings Selected by Ursula King.* Maryknoll, N.Y.: Orbis, 1999.

Descartes, Rene. *Meditations on First Philosophy.* Ronald Rubin, trans. Claremont, Calif.: Arete, 1986.

Dooley, Thomas. *Deliver Us from Evil.* New York: Farrar, Straus and Cudahy, 1956.

_____. *The Edge of Tomorrow.* New York: Farrar, Straus and Cudahy, 1958.

_____. *The Night They Burned the Mountain.* New York: Farrar, Straus and Cudahy, 1960.

Dougherty, Luke. *Tending the Soul.* Unpublished manuscript.

_____. *Tending the Soul: Learnings from a Lifetime of Spiritual Direction.* Centralia, Wash.: RPI, 2007.

Dupre, Louis and James Wiseman. *Light from Light: An Anthology of Christian Mysticism.* Mahwah, N.J.: Paulist, 2001.

Einstein, Albert. *Ideas and Opinions.* Sonja Bargmann, trans. New York: Random House, 1954.

_____. *The World As I See It.* Filiquarian, 2006.

Ellsberg, Robert. *All Saints: Daily Reflections on Saints, Prophets, and Witnesses for Our Time.* New York: Crossroad, 2000.

_____. *Charles de Foucauld*. Maryknoll, N.Y.: Orbis, 1999

Farrow, John. *Damien the Leper*. New York: Image, 1954.

Gandhi, M.K., *An Autobiography: The Story of My Experiments with Truth*. Boston: Beacon, 1957.

Gawande, Atul. *Complications: The Surgeon's Notes on an Imperfect Science*. New York: Metropolitan, 2002.

Gonzales-Balado, Jose Luis. *Mother Teresa, In My Own Words*. New York: Gramercy Random House, 1996.

Gonzales-Balado, Jose Luis. *Heart of Joy*. Ann Arbor, Mich.: Servant, 1987.

Hardick, Lothar. *The Admonitions of St. Francis of Assisi*. David Smith, trans. Chicago: Franciscan Herald, 1982.

Hutchinson, Gloria. *Six Ways to Pray from Six Great Saints*. Cincinnati: St. Anthony Messenger Press, 1982.

Isaacson, Walter. *Einstein: His Life and Universe*. New York: Simon and Schuster, 2007.

Kavanaugh, Kieran and Otilio Rodriguez. *The Collected Works of St. John of the Cross*. Washington, D.C.: ICS, 1991.

_____. trans., *The Collected Works of St. Teresa of Avila*, Washington, D.C.: ICS, 1987.

à Kempis, Thomas. *The Imitation of Christ*. New York: Penguin, 1952.

_____. *My Imitation of Christ*. John J. Gorman, trans. Brooklyn, N.Y.: Confraternity of the Precious Blood, 1954.

Lawrence, Elliot. *I Will Be Called John: A Biography of Pope John XXIII*. New York: E. P. Dutton, 1973.

Liguori, Alphonsus. *Preparation for Death or Considerations on the Eternal Truths*. Eugene Grimm, ed. Brooklyn, N.Y.: Redemptorist, 1926.

Martin, James. *My Life with the Saints*. Chicago: Loyola, 2006.

Merton, Thomas. *Thoughts in Solitude*. New York: Farrar, Straus and Giroux, 1956.

Mother Teresa and Brother Roger. *Seeking the Heart of God: Reflections on Prayer*. San Francisco: HarperSanFrancisco, 1991.

Mother Teresa, *Essential Writings*. Jean Maalouf, ed. Maryknoll, N.Y.: Orbis, 2001.

Newman, John Henry. *Selected Sermons, Prayers, and Devotions*. John F. Thornton and Susan B. Varenne, eds. New York: Vintage, 1999.

O'Rourke, Kevin D., and Philip Boyle. *Medical Ethics: Sources of Catholic Teachings.* Washington, D.C.: Georgetown University Press, 1999.

Pope John XXIII. *Journal of a Soul.* Dorothy White, trans. New York: McGraw-Hill, 1965.

Royle, Roger and Gary Woods, *Mother Teresa: A Life in Pictures.* New York: Harper Collins, 1992.

Schweitzer, Albert. "Aus Meinem Leben und Denken" *My Life & Thought: An Autobiography.* C. T. Campion, trans. New York: Henry Holt, 1933.

_____. *The Philosophy of Civilization.* C.T. Campion, trans. New York: Macmillan, 1949.

Thérèse of Lisieux. *The Story of a Soul.* New York: Image, 1957.

_____. *The Story of A Soul.* Robert J. Edmonson, trans. and ed. Brewster, Mass.: Paraclete, 2006.

_____. *Her Last Conversations.* John Clarke, trans. Washington, D.C.: ICS, 1977.

Thurston, H. J., and D. Attwater. *Butler's Lives of the Saints,* South Bend, Ind.: Ave Maria, 1956.

Treece, Paticia. *Mornings with Thérèse of Lisieux.* Ann Arbor, Mich.: Servant, 1997.

Von Speyr, Adrienne. *They Followed his Call: Vocation and Asceticism.* San Francisco: Ignatius, 1986..

_____. *The Christian State of Life.* Hans Urs von Balthasar, ed., and Mary Frances McCarthy, trans. San Francisco: Ignatius, 1986.

Periodicals

Dooley, Tom. "Letter to Father Hesburgh" UNDR 20/10, Box 20, Folder 10, Notre Dame Miscellaneous University Records, Archives of the University of Notre Dame.

Drake, Tim. "Mother of the Family: Pope to canonize doctor who died for her daughter." *National Catholic Register.*

Feister, John Bookser. "Cardinal Joseph L. Bernardin: Didn't He Show Us the Way?" *St. Anthony Messenger,* February, 1997.

Forest, Jim. "What I learned about justice from Dorothy Day." *Claretian,* 1996.

Healy, Bernardine. "Teaming Up." *US News & World Report,* January 23, 2005.

Hobson, Katherine. "Doctors Vanish from View." *U.S. News & World Report*, January 13, 2005.

Pope John XXIII. "On Succeeding Pius XII," *Time*, February 1, 1960.

Weigel, George. "Perspectives: A Patron Saint for Life." *The Southern Cross*, May 20, 2004.

White, Kate "The hidden life of Charles de Foucauld." *National Catholic Reporter*, November 11, 2005.

Web Sites

American Catholic: http://www.AmericanCatholic.org.

Catholic Destination: http://www.catholicdestination.com.

Catholic Information Network: http://www.cin.org.

The Catholic Encyclopedia: http://www.newadvent.org.

The Catholic Forum: http://www.catholic-forum.com.

Catholic Online: http://www.catholic.org.

The Catholic Worker: http://www.catholicworker.org.

Christianity Today International: http://www.christianitytoday.com.

Daily Catholic: http://www.dailycatholic.org.

The Secular Franciscan Home Page: http://secularfranciscans.org.

The Vatican Official Web site: http://www.vatican.va.

INDEX

abortion, Gianna Molla's refusal of,
20
accomplishments, reflecting on, 82
*Act of Consecration to the Immaculate
Heart of Mary*, 97
Africa, Albert Schweitzer's work in,
66, 67–68
anastomosis, 135–136
anger, apologizing for, 35
Arcolino, Elisabeth, 20–21
arrogance, 55
assassination, of Archbishop Oscar
Romero, 50
atheism, 89
atonement, 65

Bernadin, Cardinal Joseph, 21–24
books, 152–156
brain, complexities and difficulties in
understanding, 18
brain damage, 18
Bresslau, Helene, 66

Calcutta, Mother Teresa in, 11–13
Camillus de Lellis, Saint, 103–105
capitalism, impact on medicine, 1–3,
46, 64, 139–141
Carmelite Order
convent in Lisieux, 30,
32–33
Saint John of the Cross
recruited to, 90

and Saint Teresa of Avila,
112–115
Carrel, Alexis, 135–136
Catherine of Siena, Saint, 32
Catholic Worker movement,
147–149
centering prayer. *See* contemplative
prayer
*The Challenge of Peace: God's Promise
and Our Response*, 21–22
charity
Saint Camillus de Lellis as
exemplar, 103–105
Saint Vincent de Paul as
exemplar, 100–103
China, Pierre Teilhard de Chardin
"exiled" to, 133–134
Christ
Mother Teresa radiating love
of, 10
seeing, in patients, 13
seeing, in poor patients, 149
*Christianity and the Religions of the
World*, 67
Civilization and Ethics, 67
clerical abuse, Cardinal Bernadin's
stance on, 23
coma
decisions with, 18, 24
miraculous recovery from,
73–76

compassion, exemplified by Mother
    Teresa of Calcutta, 10–13
*Complications: The Surgeon's Notes on
    an Imperfect Science*, 109
Confessions (Saint Augustine), 113
Congregation of the Mission, estab-
    lishment by Saint Vincent de
    Paul, 101
Congregation of the Oratory,
    126–127
contemplation in action
    Brother Lawrence as exem-
        plar, 39–42
    Saint John of God as exem-
        plar, 42–44
contemplative prayer, 37–38
control, surgeon's, 105–110
controversy
    in Dorothy Day's early life,
        145–148
    over Teilhard de Chardin's
        theological ideas,
        133–134
convents, established by Saint Teresa
    of Avila, 115
conversion
    Adrienne von Speyr's, 95
    Blessed Charles de
        Foucauld's, 57
    Dorothy Day's, into authentic
        Christianity, 147
conversos, 112
Cope, Blessed Marianne, 60–61, 144
"Cosmic Life," 133
courage
    Archbishop Oscar Arnulfo
        Romero as exemplar,
        48–50
    Saint Maximilian Kolbe as
        exemplar, 47–48

Daughters of Charity, 102
Day, Dorothy, 145–149
de Chardin, Pierre Teilhard, 132–135
"A Declaration of Conscience," 68

de Foucauld, Blessed Charles, 56–60
Deliver Us From Evil, 79
Discalced Carmelite Nuns of the
    Primitive Rule of Saint Joseph at
    Avila, 115
discipline, 63–64
    Albert Schweitzer as exem-
        plar, 64–68
    Saint Elizabeth of Hungary as
        exemplar, 68–70
divine providence, trust in
    Pope John XXIII as exemplar,
        116–119
    Saint Teresa of Avila as exem-
        plar, 111–116
Dooley, Tom, 78–82

The Edge of Tomorrow, 81
Elizabeth of Hungary, Saint, 68–70
El Salvador, and Archbishop Oscar
    Romero, 48–50
entitlement, feelings of, 61
ethics
    Cardinal Joseph Bernadin as
        exemplar, 21–24
    Gianna Beretta Molla as
        exemplar, 19–21
    as "seamless garment," 22
ethics committees, 19, 24
exclaustration,11
extraordinary measures, 19

faith
    Adrienne von Speyr as exem-
        plar, 93–96
    Saint John of the Cross as
        exemplar, 89–93
    trials of, 96
faith, and academics
    Alexis Carrel's balancing,
        135–136
    Pierre Teilhard de Chardin's
        balancing, 132–135
Fathers of a Good Death, establish-
    ment of, 104

fortitude
 Archbishop Oscar Arnulfo
  Romero as exemplar,
  48–50
 Saint Maximilian Kolbe as
  exemplar, 47–48

Garrone, Evaristo, 128
Gawande, Atul, 109
Genesis of a Thought, 133
God
 believing in, 88–89
 as main surgeon, 110
 subservience to, 105
 trust in, 41–42, 119
 See also Christ
Gonxha, Agnes. See Teresa, Mother
Grande, Father Rutilio, 49–50

Hans Urs von Balthasar, Father,
 95–96
Hansen, Gerhard Henrick Armauer,
 143
Hawaii, mission work in, 143
healthcare system
 complexities and problems,
  139–141
 paradigm shift in, 1–3
healthcare workers, necessary quali-
 ties, 3
Herman, Nicholas. See Lawrence,
 Brother
hermit, Charles de Foucauld as, 58
honesty
 Cardinal Joseph Bernadin as
  exemplar, 21–24
 Gianna Beretta Molla as
  exemplar, 19–21
hope
 Saint Luke the Evangelist as
  exemplar, 76–78
 Tom Dooley as exemplar,
  78–82
hospitals, founders of
 Albert Schweitzer, 66–67

Blessed Marianne Cope, 61
Tom Dooley, 80–81
Saint Elizabeth of Hungary,
 69
Saint John of God, 43
Saint Vincent de Paul, 102
humanism
 and medicine, link between,
  87
 Saint Camillus de Lellis as
  exemplar, 103–105
 Saint Vincent de Paul as
  exemplar, 100–103
humility, 54–55
 Blessed Charles de Foucauld
  as exemplar, 56–60
 Blessed Marianne Cope as
  exemplar, 60–61
 learning through erring, 109
humor, sense of
 Blessed Artemide Zatti as
  exemplar, 127–129
 Saint Philip Neri as exemplar, 124–127

idealism
 giving way to callousness,
  7–9, 13
 and medicine, link between,
  87
illness, trusting in God during,
 41–42
Immaculata movement, founded by
 Saint Maximilian Kolbe, 47
imprisonment, of Saint John of the
 Cross, 91
Incarnation convent, 112–113
initiative
 Albert Schweitzer as exemplar, 64–68
 Saint Elizabeth of Hungary as
  exemplar, 68–70
"inner necessity," 70
integrity

Cardinal Joseph Bernadin as
exemplar, 21–24
Gianna Beretta Molla as
exemplar, 19–21
intensive care unit (ICU), difficult
decisions in, 15–19
interfaith dialogue, Pope John XXIII
and, 117
The Interior Castle, 114

John of God, Saint, 42–44
John of the Cross, Saint, 89–93
John XXIII, Pope, 116–119
Journal of a Soul, 116

kindness, exemplified by Mother
Teresa of Calcutta, 10–13
The Knight of the Immaculata, 47

Ladies of Charity, 102
Lambaréné, Albert Schweitzer's work
in, 66, 67–68
Lawrence, Brother, 39–42
Lazarists. *See* Padres Paules
leadership
Albert Schweitzer as exemplar, 64–68
Saint Elizabeth of Hungary as
exemplar, 68–70
lepers
Blessed Damien of Molokai
caring for, 142, 143–145
Blessed Marianne Cope's
work with, 60–61
hospital for, begun by Albert
Schweitzer, 67
liberation theology, 49–50, 118
life, laying down, for beliefs, 47–50
lifeline, to take stock of significant
times and people, 82–84
Little Brothers of Jesus, 59
love
Saint Camillus de Lellis as
exemplar, 103–105

Saint Vincent de Paul as
exemplar, 100–103
Ludwig of Hungary, 68–69
Luke the Evangelist, Saint, 76–78

malpractice insurance, 140–141
managed care, paradigm shift to, 1–3
Martin, Louis and Zélie, 32–33
Maximilian Kolbe, Saint, 47–48
Medical International Cooperation
Organization. *See* MEDICO
medical school, drop in applications,
2
medicine
decisions usurped from medical professionals, 64
as humbling profession,
54–55
as lifelong study, 54
and religion, link between,
45–46
simple days of, 45
and spirituality, link between,
87
See also nursing,
physician(s), surgery
MEDICO, 81
mental institutions, established by
Saint Vincent de Paul, 102
Ministers of the Sick, 105
miracles
attributed to Saint Elizabeth
of Hungary, 70
Saint John of God, 43
misdiagnoses, frequency of, 55–56,
109
missionaries, established by Saint
Vincent de Paul, 102
Missionaries of Charity, 10
Molla, Gianna Beretta, 19–21
Molokai, treating lepers on, 143
motivation, 105
mystical visions
Adrienne von Speyr's, 94,
95–95

Saint John of God's, 43
Saint Teresa of Avila's, 114

Nazis, murder of Saint Maximilian
Kolbe by, 47–48
The Night They Burned the Mountain,
81
"noosphere," 133, 134
nuclear weapons, and Albert
Schweitzer, 68
nursing
Blessed Marianne Cope's high
standards for, 61
Dorothy Day's foray into,
146–147
Mother Teresa trained in, 12
Saint Camillus's exceptional
skill in, 104–105

*On the Edge of the Primeval Forest: The
Decay and Restoration of
Civilization*, 67
orphanages, Saint Vincent de Paul,
102

Pacem in Terris, 116–117
Padres Paules, 101
patience
with difficult families, 30
exemplified by Saint Thérèse
of Lisieux, 30–34
patient(s)
becoming callous toward,
7–9
difficulties with families,
29–30
keeping code going for, 63
taking time with families,
16–18, 24
Paul, Saint, and Saint Luke, 77–78
Peace or Atomic War?, 68
periodicals, 156
perseverance
Saint Luke the Evangelist as
exemplar, 76–78

Tom Dooley as exemplar,
78–82
Philip Neri, Saint, 124–127
physician(s)
attitude toward loss, 15
financial burdens on,
140
Saint Luke the Evangelist as,
77
physician burn-out, 2, 46–47
poor
problems with serving,
139–140
serving, 141
urban, 148–149
Vincent de Paul's commit-
ment to, 101–103
working with, 149
See also preferential option
for the poor
practicality
Blessed Artemide Zatti as
exemplar, 127–129
Saint Philip Neri as exemplar, 124–127
The Practice of the Presence of God, 39,
40
prayer(s), 13–14, 24, 35, 44, 51, 70,
84–85 129, 137, 150
Act of Consecration to the
Immaculate Heart of
Mary, 97
before surgery, 38–39
contemplative, 37–38
four stages of, 114–115
frequency of, 44
The Prayer of Abandonment
of Brother Charles of
Jesus, 120
My Prayer Before Making
Rounds, 106
Prayer of the Little Brothers
and Sisters of Jesus, 62
prayer group, contemplative, 37–38

prayer life, Saint Teresa's struggles with, 113–114
preaching, inappropriateness of, 58–59
preferential option for the poor, 118
   and Archbishop Oscar Romero, 49, 50
   Blessed Damien of Molokai as exemplar, 142–145
   Dorothy Day as exemplar, 145–149
prison, Dorothy Day's work in, 148–149
pro-life ideology, 20–22
providence, divine, trust in,
   Pope John XXIII as exemplar, 116–119
   Saint Teresa of Avila as exemplar, 111–116

The Quest for the Historical Jesus, 65

racism, making atonement for, 65
"recipe medicine," 1
reformation, Carmelite, 90–92
religion, and science, 131–133
   Alexis Carrel's balancing of, 135–136
   link between, 45–46
   Pierre Teilhard de Chardin's balancing of, 132–135
responsibility
   Albert Schweitzer as exemplar, 64–68
   Saint Elizabeth of Hungary as exemplar, 68–70
"Reverence for Life," 67
Rome, Saint Philip Neri's work in, 125–126
Romero, Archbishop Oscar Arnulfo, 48–50
Roncalli, Angelo. See John XXIII, Pope

sacrifice, 110–111

saints, reaction to modern-day medicine, 4–5, 141–142
Salesian Order, and Artemide Zatti, 127–128
school, girls', opened by Blessed Marianne Cope, 61
Schweitzer, Albert, 64–68
science, and religion, 131–136
service, inconvenience of, 99–100
slaves, liberating, 102
social justice
   Blessed Damien of Molokai as exemplar, 142–145
   Cardinal Bernadin's commitment to, 22–24
   Dorothy Day as exemplar, 145–149
   and economic justice, 141
socialist, Dorothy Day as, 146–149
The Spirit of the Earth, 134
spiritual director, Brother Lawrence as, 40–42
Spiritual Energy of Suffering, 134
spirituality
   Adrienne von Speyr as exemplar, 93–96
   and medicine, link between, 87
   Saint John of the Cross as exemplar, 89–93
spirituality, and technology
   Alexis Carrel's balancing of, 135–136
   Pierre Teilhard de Chardin's balancing of, 132–135
The Spiritual Phenomenon, 134
The Spiritual Power of Matter, 133
Story of a Soul, 30–31
surgery
   art and science of, 107–109
   complications following, 17–18
   praying before, 38–39
sympathy, exemplified by Mother Teresa of Calcutta, 10–13

temper, losing, 35
temperance
Blessed Charles de Foucauld
as exemplar, 56–60
Blessed Marianne Cope as
exemplar, 60–61
Tending the Soul, 82
Tercer Abecedario, 113
Teresa of Avila, Saint, 32, 111–116
and Saint John of the Cross,
90–91
Teresa of Calcutta, Mother, 4–5, 7,
10–13
therapeutic abortion, Gianna Molla's
refusal of, 20
Thérèse of Lisieux, Saint, 30–34
tolerance, exemplified by Saint
Thérèse of Lisieux, 30–34
tragedy, being able to see beyond,
88–89
trauma
balancing multiple cases,
28–30

miraculous recovery from,
73–76
tuberculosis, being cured through
prayer, 128

understanding, exemplified by Saint
Thérèse of Lisieux, 30–34

vascular research, by Alexis Carrel,
135–136
Vatican II, 118
Vespers/Compline, praying regularly,
38
Vigils/Lauds, praying regularly, 38
Vincent de Paul, Saint, 100–103
Vincentians. See Padres Paules
von Speyr, Adrienne, 93–96

Way of Perfection, 114
Web sites, 156–157

Zatti, Blessed Artemide, 127–129